THE MOST DANGEROUS MAN IN THE WORLD:

DAWOOD IBRAHIM

THE MOST DANGEROUS MAN IN THE WORLD:
DAWOOD IBRAHIM

- Billionaire Gangster

- Protector of Osama bin Laden

- Nuclear Black Market Entrepreneur

- Islamic Extremist and Global Terrorist

Gilbert King

Chamberlain Bros.
a member of
Penguin Group (USA) Inc.

Chamberlain Bros.
a member of
Penguin Group (USA) Inc.
375 Hudson Street
New York, NY 10014

LIBRARY OF CONGRESS CATALOGING-IN-PUBLICATION DATA
King, Gilbert.
  The most dangerous man in the world : Dawood Ibrahim : billionaire gangster, protector of Osama bin Laden, nuclear black market entrepreneur, Islamic extremist and global terrorist / Gilbert King.
     p. cm.
  Includes bibliographical references.
  ISBN 1-59609-001-4
  1. Ibrahim, Dawood, 1955— 2. Terrorists—Pakistan—Biography. 3. Terrorists—India—Biography. 4. Gangsters—Pakistan—Biography. 5. Terrorism—India. I. Title.
  HV6430.I27K56 2004   2004007452
  303.6'25'092—dc22

Printed in the United States of America

1 3 5 7 9 10 8 6 4 2

Book designed by Mike Rivilis.

CONTENTS

Dawood Ibrahim is the

Osama bin Laden

of South Asia.

INTRODUCTION

Aside from September 11th, 2001, Dawood Ibrahim is responsible for the greatest act of terrorism in the world: He masterminded the Bombay serial blasts in 1993, which killed approximately three hundred people and injured over a thousand more. Dawood is the Osama bin Laden of South Asia, but, unlike bin Laden, he lives like a king in his mansion in Karachi, Pakistan, while bin Laden moves from cave to cave in the dark of night. And while bin Laden sleeps on dusty, insect-ridden floors, and, according to some reports, often is attached to a kidney dialysis machine, Dawood sleeps until noon, often waking up with Karachi's youngest and most beautiful just-deflowered virgins by his side. Although the two terrorists are often linked because of their wealth and their willingness to use their resources to further the Islamic extremist agenda, it is Osama bin Laden who gets most of the attention. And Dawood Ibrahim would like to keep it that way. Despite the fact that both bin Laden and Ibrahim have been designated "global terrorists" by the United States

Treasury Department, and both easily make the short list for the most wanted men in the world, the differences between the two are startling.

Financially, bin Laden is a pauper by comparison. Dawood Ibrahim controls the largest drug smuggling routes in an area that produces more than 75 percent of the world's heroin. On top of that, he owns and operates multinational companies, both legal and illegal, from South Asia to Europe, dealing weapons, drugs, gold, and real estate. He formed his own gang in India, "D Company," which grew into a meganetwork and remains one of the deadliest and most politically connected organized crime outfits in the world. Through D Company, Ibrahim is said to control most betting on cricket matches, and he has established himself as a major financier of Bollywood films. And recent events in Pakistan involving the nuclear black market and Dr. A. Q. Khan's confession regarding the transport of enriched uranium and missiles hint at Dawood's involvement.

When Osama bin Laden needed help evading U.S. forces after the invasion of Afghanistan, he turned to Dawood Ibrahim, who reportedly negotiated a financial arrangement allowing bin Laden to use his smuggling routes along the Pakistani/Afghan border. But while bin Laden must depend on the loyalty of his al-Qaeda operatives for protection, Ibrahim has a much more powerful team watching his back—Pakistan's

Inter-Services Intelligence (ISI) agency. Together, the ISI and Dawood Ibrahim have been partners in a mutually beneficial relationship dating back to 1993, when Dawood agreed, at the ISI's behest, to strike back at India for allowing communal riots to occur after the Babri Masjid mosque in Bombay was demolished by more than a million protesting Hindis. The riots claimed the lives of hundreds of Muslims and destroyed *crores'* worth of Muslim property. Just a few months later, Dawood began sending his men to train in weapon detonation facilities in Pakistan and Afghanistan, then brought them back to Bombay to wreak havoc on the city.

Since then, Dawood Ibrahim has been forced to live in Pakistan, protected by the ISI, where he continues to provide financial support to terrorist groups working against Indian interests, and to facilitate espionage operation for Pakistan by extorting and bribing Indian officials through his still prosperous and influential D Company. The ISI, in return, has not only protected Ibrahim, but allowed him to establish an underworld empire in Karachi. Dawood is believed to control the city's gunrunning business, the stock exchange, and *hundi*, the parallel credit system business, in addition to the many real estate holdings he maintains in the city. In Karachi, Dawood lives like a king. According to Ghulam Hasnain's "Portrait of a Don," which ran in *Newsline* magazine, the popular Pakistan weekly, Dawood is also supporting the local pimps of Karachi with his voracious sexual appetite. A family friend is quoted in Hasnain's article as saying, "He prefers virgins, preferably young girls. And he is a good paymaster. If the market rate for a woman is 10,000 rupees, Dawood pays 100,000 rupees. He is thus always surrounded by Pakistan's top call girls."

Hasnain describes the activities in Ibrahim's eighteen-thousand-square-foot Karachi mansion—with its pool, tennis courts, snooker room, and hi-tech gym—where Bollywood actresses are flown in for lavish parties. "They wouldn't dare refuse an invitation," says one of Dawood's friends. And friends are what he has plenty of in Karachi. He is said to employ numerous government undercover agents and former ISI officials, who, according to some of Hasnain's sources, are more loyal to Dawood than they are to the government of Pakistan.

Conservative estimates put Dawood Ibrahim's personal net worth at more than a billion dollars, but the amount he contributes each year to ISI alone is rumored to exceed a billion. He is believed to have bailed out Pakistan's Central Bank during a crisis in 2000, and at a time when no country in the world had more sanctions leveled against it, Pakistan was still able to fund and purchase nuclear technology on the black market.

Dawood Ibrahim, who rose from Bombay street urchin to undisputed leader of one of the largest crime networks the world has ever seen, remains to this day a mysterious and very dangerous man. Wanted by India for well over a decade, and now by the United States for his al-Qaeda connections, Ibrahim has been able to elude his would-be captors by manipulating relationships with various governments, including Pakistan and the United Arab Emirates. Some say he is the ultimate twenty-first-century businessman, ruthlessly aggressive with competitors yet generously loyal to those on his team. Others say he is nothing but a terrorist and the scourge of the earth. Either way, he is a force to be reckoned with. With unlimited financial resources and a proven willingness to use mass terror to achieve his objectives, Dawood Ibrahim is the most dangerous man in the world.

On October 16, 2003,

the U.S. Treasury Department

designated Dawood Ibrahim as a

global terrorist with links

to al-Qaeda.

CHAPTER ONE

THE KING OF KARACHI: DANIEL PEARL AND THE MOST DANGEROUS MAN IN THE WORLD

In January 2002, Daniel Pearl, a reporter with the *Wall Street Journal*, was in Pakistan working on a story about Richard C. Reid, the "shoe bomber" who attempted to ignite some plastic explosives hidden in his sneakers while on an American Airlines flight from Paris to Miami. Reid had been found to have connections to the Muslim militant group *Jamaat ul-Fuqra* ("The Impoverished") in Pakistan, and Pearl, during the course of his investigation, began to uncover information that he felt raised more questions than answers. Reid was being held without bail in the United States, but Pearl wondered just who Reid might have been working for, and some of the signs seemed to point in the direction of terrorist groups with known connections to Pakistan's Inter-Services Intelligence (ISI).

While in Karachi, Daniel Pearl had read a piece by the Pakistani newspaper writer Ghulam Hasnain about the former Bombay mafia head, Dawood Ibrahim, who was now living in Pakistan under the protection of the ISI. Hasnain's cover story in *Newsline*, a respected Pakistani monthly, entitled "Portrait of a Don," was an exposé on Dawood's life of excess in Karachi. His story gave specifics about Dawood's organized crime dealings around the world, his penchant for prostitutes, and the murders of those who crossed him. The story fascinated Pearl, and he was eager to write a story of his own about the man now known as the "King of Karachi." According to Robert Sam Anson in his *Vanity Fair* story "The Journalist and the Terrorist," Pearl called an associate, Ikram Sehgal, for leads on Dawood.

"He asked if I had any contacts with the local Mafia. I said, 'Danny, the Mafia head here doesn't function the way you think Mafias do. This is not something out of *The Godfather*. I know the direction you're going in. Don't do this! Forget it. If you want to know something, come over and we'll talk, not on the telephone."

A few days later, Pearl spoke with the Dow Jones correspondent in Karachi, Saaed Azhari, who told him there was something he ought to know: Hasnain, the author of the Dawood piece Pearl had admired, had disappeared. It would turn out he had been picked up by the ISI and was released two days later—but not until "after they got a suicide note signed from him," according to a well-informed Pakistani journalist. It is believed that Hasnain was so traumatized by his "interrogation" that he has yet to speak publicly about it.

The day after Hasnain's disappearance, Daniel Pearl himself vanished after attempting to meet a contact who was going to introduce him to key figures in the Karachi underworld. Instead, he is believed to have met Mansur Hasnain, a known terrorist, in the Village Garden Restaurant. The drama of Pearl's kidnapping played out over the next few weeks as a group called The National Movement for the Restoration of Pakistani Sovereignty e-mailed photographs of Pearl in captivity to Western news outlets, along with a list of demands that included U.S.-made F-16 fighter jets and access to Pakistani nationals held in Guantanamo Bay, Cuba.

These demands, of course, were never met, and it is believed that when news of Daniel Pearl's Jewish background was leaked by the Pakistani media, he was murdered. An investigation was immediately launched at the highest level of the Pakistani government, and once it was learned that extremists with links to al-Qaeda may have been involved, Pakistan's president General Pervez Musharraf made an off-the-cuff remark at an impromptu press conference regarding the murder that remains puzzling to this day. "Unfortunately," he said, Pearl had become "overly inquisitive."

According to Siddharth Varadarajan, in a story from the Times News Network, "many local journalists feel Pearl had stumbled across information which might have embarrassed the Inter-Services Intelligence agency in some way." Indeed, much of the evidence in the Pearl case would point to Saeed Ahmed Sheikh, a known terrorist in Pakistan who would later confess to his involvement in the abduction. Oddly, Sheikh spent a week in ISI custody before he was turned in to Pakistani authorities. He told police and the FBI apparently everything he knew about the kidnapping of Daniel Pearl, but one subject was off-limits—that week he spent with the ISI. "I know people in the government," was all he would say, "and they know me and my work."

What exactly did President Musharraf mean when he casually mentioned that Pearl had become overly inquisitive? Varadarajan, in his piece, quotes a senior columnist for *Jang*, the Urdu daily: "We can only presume he [Pearl] came close to finding out the roots of some people with the ISI." Indeed, during the U.S. war on Afghanistan, it is believed that more than three thousand Western journalists passed through Pakistan. Why, exactly, was Pearl singled out?

The answer may well be the questions Daniel Pearl was asking about organized crime in Karachi, and, specifically, about Dawood Ibrahim. After all, the one thing Pearl shared in common with Ghulam Hasnain, the other journalist "picked up" around the same time in Karachi, was a keen interest in telling Dawood Ibrahim's story. It is understandable why Pakistan would be leery of any Western reporters poking around the former don from Bombay. In the war against terror, it is Osama bin Laden who garners all the attention from the West, and Pakistan would just as soon keep it that way. In spite of the fact that most evidence suggests that the head of al-Qaeda has been hiding in that country, the Pakistani government can at least save face by claiming that he is not welcome there, and that the United States is welcome to join the search for him.

But with Dawood Ibrahim, it is an entirely different matter. He is India's version of Osama bin Laden, only smarter, richer, and more deadly. Most important, however, he is an "honored guest" in Pakistan. He's been issued several passports, and he is protected by the ISI. It is common knowledge that Karachi has been offered as a safe haven to him because of his value to Pakistan. Ever since he masterminded the 1993 Bombay serial blasts, a deadly attack in that bustling city, Dawood has turned against India, providing the ISI with invaluable intelligence and allowing the agency use of his hit men and terrorist connections to get back at his onetime homeland.

Aside from providing intelligence, Dawood Ibrahim has provided financial support to the ISI. It is estimated that he contributes over $1 billion annually in exchange for protection and freedom to run his empire from Karachi. But Dawood's generosity does not end there. When Pakistan's Central Bank was in crisis in 2000, it is believed that he "loaned" the bank millions. However, business was going so well in Karachi for him that later reports suggested that he no longer considered his bank bailout a loan but a "donation" instead, a gesture of goodwill aimed at solidifying the assurances he received from the ISI that he could continue managing his empire without interference.

After Dawood Ibrahim was forced to abandon India as his home, there was some question as to whether he would be able to maintain his network. In fact, he continues to conduct significant business in India from Pakistan, both legal and illegal. His net worth, conservatively estimated several years ago at over $1 billion, encompasses interests in Malaysia, Singapore, Sri Lanka, Dubai, France, Germany, and the United Kingdom, not to mention Muslim countries in Africa. But whatever money he may have lost when fleeing Bombay he easily offset on moving to Pakistan by gaining control of the real estate market, the stock exchanges, and gunrunning interests in Karachi. And there is no question that his profits from controlling the major drug smuggling routes along the Pakistani/Afghan border, a region that produces 75 percent of the world's opium, have helped Dawood climb higher on the list of the world's richest people. Ironically, after the Taliban was removed from power in Afghanistan, victorious warlords from the Northern Alliance saw to it that farmers began planting opium at unprecedented levels in the region. The United States' Central Intelligence Agency, aware of this opium boom, has been willing to look the other way in exchange for support in the war on terror. Today, heroin continues to be produced in record volume, and it is believed that Ibrahim's take from these profits is significant.

On October 16, 2003, the U.S. Treasury Department designated Dawood Ibrahim as a global terrorist with links to al-Qaeda after it learned that he had reached a financial agreement with Osama bin Laden for bin Laden's use of Ibrahim's smuggling routes in South Asia, the Middle East, and Africa. In effect, Osama had turned to Dawood for help to avoid capture after the U.S. invaded Afghanistan, and Dawood delivered. Since then, Dawood has heavily funded an Islamic militant group known as "Army of the Righteous," a.k.a. *Lashkar-e-Tayyiba* (LeT), despite the fact that this group was banned by the Pakistani government after several vicious and deadly terrorist attacks in India.

After the events of 9/11, Colin Powell, U.S. Secretary of State, met with President Musharraf in an attempt to persuade Pakistan to turn Dawood Ibrahim over to India after India released its infamous list of twenty fugitives being sheltered in Pakistan. "We hope," Powell said, "Musharraf will examine all the information and do what is proper in the case of each of the twenty individuals." Powell had received assurances from India that it would remove its troops from the Pakistan border once Pakistan handed over the criminals, and Dawood Ibrahim was at the top of the list. It was an important moment for the U.S. administration in its attempt to align its allies in the war against terror.

However, the answer Powell received could not have been more disappointing to both him and India. According to Pakistan information minister Sheikh Rashid Ahmed, Dawood—the man they called the "King of Karachi"—was not there. "He is neither a Pakistani citizen, nor does he live in Karachi. If somebody is aware of his whereabouts, we will receive and act on that information." Ahmed went on: "The Pakistan Government has nothing to do with people being identified as members of the underworld."

That same day, the United States released Dawood's Karachi address, eight telephone numbers used by him, and the identification numbers on nine of Dawood's Pakistani passports. This "fact sheet" also specifically listed Dawood's links to drug smuggling networks, terrorist organizations, Osama bin Laden, and the Taliban. But what wasn't listed in the fact sheet was even more frightening and has only recently come to light.

In February 2004, Dr. Abdul Qadeer Khan, a top Pakistani

scientist, "father of Pakistan's nuclear bomb," and national hero, addressed the nation on television and admitted he used a "nuclear black market" to sell technology to Iran, Libya, and North Korea. President Musharraf made the following statement: "Pakistan, as a state, never has and never will proliferate its hard earned nuclear technology to any other country. What unfortunately happened in the past, from 1989 to 1999, were individual actions based on personal greed and gross misuse of autonomy and authority; it was a betrayal of the nation's trust, it was compounded by an ineffective and inefficient security system, and an absence of institutionalized oversight. These individuals were subverted from within. Nevertheless, this aberration too was checked when institutional arrangements were put in place in 2000."

A week later, Khan was officially pardoned by Musharraf. The CIA had already gathered unassailable evidence that Musharraf was aware Pakistan was using U.S.-supplied C-130 transport aircraft to fly Nodong missiles from North Korea to the A. Q. Khan research laboratories. What concerned officials, however, was Khan's use of transnational criminal syndicates out of Dubai to move nuclear components. Most of the components sent to Libya, North Korea, and Iran were transferred through dummy companies in Dubai, exactly the type of companies Dawood had set up in the city for his arms and drug smuggling networks. Khan would later admit that he sold nuclear secrets strictly for personal profit, but intelligence experts familiar with Pakistan's politics and the ISI are highly skeptical that Khan suddenly had become an independent rogue, operating out of greed alone. His contacts with the notorious black market nuclear dealer Bukhary Seyed Abu Tahir were well documented. Tahir, whom President Bush referred to in a speech at the National Defense University of Washington, D.C., as the "chief financial officer and money launderer" of A. Q. Khan's operations, was also no stranger to Dawood Ibrahim.

Aside from his business interests in Dubai, Dawood is well entrenched in both Singapore and Malaysia. According to an article by B. Raman, and first reported to the South Asia Analysis Group in 2001, while Musharraf was on a visit to India the ISI secretly sent Dawood to Malaysia, where he stayed as Tahir's guest.

The CIA believes Dawood played an extensive role in helping Pakistan with nuclear and missile establishments, particularly because of his clandestine shipping activities and his relationships with Tahir and the ISI.

Could it be that Daniel Pearl had learned of some of the murkier connections between Dawood Ibrahim and the ISI before he was abducted and murdered? What young American reporter in Karachi wouldn't want to chase a story like Dawood's? Wouldn't he be incredulous to learn that a man who arguably controlled the largest crime network in the world—a global terrorist—was brokering nuclear secrets on the black market with the full complicity of Pakistan's ISI? It's hard to know exactly what Pearl had in mind when he showed up at the Village Garden Restaurant for an interview about organized crime in Pakistan. But it is clear that what little Pearl knew about Dawood Ibrahim, and the direction he was going with the story, ultimately may have led to his death. At some point, it must have struck Pearl as ironic that the man the world was after, Osama bin Laden, was holed up in a cave somewhere, while Dawood Ibrahim was living his life as the King of Karachi.

On March 12, 1993, the day now known as "Black Friday," thousands of brokers and traders were hustling into the Bombay Stock Exchange when a suicide bomber drove a car into the basement of the building and detonated an immensely powerful bomb.

CHAPTER TWO

THE ROAD TO BOMBAY: BLACK FRIDAY AND THE RISE OF DAWOOD IBRAHIM

The United States may have been caught off guard by the magnitude of the attacks on September 11, 2001, but residents of Bombay, who watched the horrific events unfold on television, were reminded of their own tragic day just eight years earlier. On March 12, 1993, the day now known as "Black Friday," thousands of brokers and traders were hustling into the Bombay Stock Exchange when a suicide bomber drove a car into the basement of the building and detonated an immensely powerful bomb. Those who survived the initial blast had little time to make sense of the destruction around them before another bomb exploded across town. And then another. And another. In all, it is believed that twelve bombs exploded in the city that day. Now referred to as the "Bombay serial blasts," the bombings were timed just minutes apart at key targets across the sprawling metropolis. When all was finally quiet again, nearly three hundred people had been killed and over a thousand injured.

The Indian government demanded answers. Who could have been behind such a vicious act of terrorism? Initial speculation pointed toward Pakistan, a likely suspect because of the ongoing conflict between the two countries over Kashmir. Others believed the serial blasts were retaliation for Babri Masjid, a mosque that was destroyed by a million-strong crowd of *karsevaks*, activists in the Vishwa Hindu Parishad (VHP, "World Hindu Council"), on December 6, 1992, which led to communal riots across India.

In the early 1980s, Bombay began to polarize in response to a severely overcrowded and underserviced population. The Shiv Sena party—the Hindu right wing—gained significant power due to its strong links to organized crime in the city. Pressure was building, and many pointed to the destruction of Babri Masjid and the subsequent rioting, deaths, and destruction of property, most of it Muslim owned, as the cause. There were reports of Muslims being shot and set ablaze on the streets, and, later, proof that the angry Hindu mobs had planned their attack of the mosque in advance and had been abetted by the police. The monthlong riots were viewed as nothing short of a "pogrom" against the Muslims, and it set in motion the retaliatory blasts that would rock Bombay just months later.

As the investigation progressed, it became clear that the major force behind the Bombay serial blasts was none other than Dawood Ibrahim, once the most powerful man in the city, at the time living in Dubai. He had been don of D Company, a ruthless organized crime outfit and an omnipotent presence in Bombay for two decades. He had his fingers in nearly every criminal enterprise in South Asia—from drug smuggling to gambling on cricket matches to fixing matches to extortion in the Bollywood film industry to the *hawala/hundi* business (a parallel credit system wherein individuals throughout Asia and the Middle East, not official banks, exchange money. It is a system used by foreign nationals sending money home to relatives, as well as by the likes of al-Qaeda to move large amounts of cash through a series of private transactions among the secret traders who operate within this kind of network)— and he never shied away from violence if it served his interests. But why would he attack Bombay?

The answers were not easy for the people of India to swallow and only confirmed their worst fears. Indeed, Pakistan was involved in the Bombay serial blasts, and indeed, the bombings were retaliatory in nature. Dawood Ibrahim masterminded the single most devastating act of terrorism India had ever seen, and that ensured that he could never return to his country. Thanks to Pakistan, however, the life of a fugitive would agree with Dawood, and, under the protection of Pakistan's ISI, he would watch his influence and his empire grow exponentially over the next decade. The man they called "Gold Man" in Bombay would quickly transform himself into the "King of Karachi," and his influence in the world's most dangerous region assured he would be courted by the likes of Osama bin Laden, Mullah Omar, and even Pakistan's president Pervez Musharraf.

Of all the rags-to-riches stories that infuse the world of Bollywood, few are more dramatic than Dawood Ibrahim's rise from street urchin to crime lord. Since the 1960s, Bombay has been one of the richest and fastest growing cities in the world, with millions flocking there to escape the poverty of the countryside. In an attempt to limit overcrowding and the usual problems that go along with it, the government inaugurated a "slum clearance" program, designing settlements intended to house up to 10 percent of the population. But the continuing migration was overwhelming Bombay and the city was unable to keep apace. The population of the city has mushroomed to over eighteen million today, and it is estimated that more than 50 percent of Bombay's people live in slums, shanties, or on the street.

Dawood Ibrahim (a.k.a. Dawood Kaskar) was born in Kher, Ratnagiri, on December 26, 1955, and grew up in

Bombay, one of millions of children who knew nothing but a future with no hope. Uneducated and illiterate, Dawood came to realize early on that crime was one way to escape his desperate situation. At some point Ibrahim Kaskar, his father, took a job as a police constable in the city, but his attempts to rescue the family from a life of poverty came too late for Dawood, who was well on his way toward his chosen profession. His father, in fact, was forced to use his position in the Criminal Investigation Division (CID) to rescue his son from a more than a few scrapes.

As Dawood grew up, so did his appetite for the "black" money (money made on the black market) that he procured on the streets of Bombay. With the collapse of the city's textile industry, Bombay had become a vision of urban despair, a perfect breeding ground for a young criminal. After committing petty theft and smuggling gold into India on Arab sailing vessels known as *dhows*, Dawood eventually traded up to crimes of a more sinister nature, while at the same time moving into legitimate business areas such as real estate. Before long, the Bombay underworld began to take notice of the ambitious young man who was quickly making a name for himself. For a brief time, he worked as an aide to Amirzada Pathan and his brother, Alamzed, who were ranking members of the Karim Lala gang. But from the start, Dawood preferred to work independently and resisted joining up permanently with any of

Bollywood world, flying movie stars into Dubai for parties everyone knew better than to decline. And over the next decade, D Company had its hands in drugs and weapons smuggling, real estate swindles, extortion, and theft.

Bollywood is all about dreams, and Dawood Ibrahim understood those dreams better than anyone.

CHAPTER THREE

THE BOLLYWOOD DREAM: BLACK MONEY AND THE INFLUENCE OF D COMPANY

Every day in India, more than ten million people pay to see a movie in one of more than thirteen thousand theaters, and, over the years, Bombay has become a virtual film factory to meet the heavy demand. More than eight hundred films are made each year in India, eight times more than in Hollywood, and they make up about a quarter of the world's film output. With poverty levels at over 50 percent in the city of Bombay alone, films lift the collective spirit of a struggling population. Bollywood is all about dreams, and Dawood Ibrahim understood those dreams better than anyone.

Until recently, the government of India would not recognize Bollywood as a legitimate industry, and banks would not make loans to producers to make movies. Clearly, there was money to be made in Bollywood, but producers were forced to turn to private financing sources, the majority of which used "black money" from the underworld. This arrangement lasted for over thirty years, dating back to mafia don Haji Mastan, who was so infatuated with an aspiring starlet that he produced films for her to star in. The problem for Bollywood has been that the underworld does not offer low-interest loans to producers, who are often in desperate need of financing once production on a film begins and money dries up due to cost overruns. Loans with 50 percent interest rates are common in the industry, with balloon payments due at any time. Threats, extortion, and murder of big Bollywood names have long been commonplace, feeding an already healthy appetite for Bollywood gossip.

With India's population nearing the one billion mark, Bollywood films are made to please a large domestic market. Sometimes called "masala movies," after the Indian dish that includes many different ingredients, the formula for these films is generally one of escapism—and there is usually something for everyone in their often three-hour running times. Action, romance, suspense, often with spectacular song-and-dance production numbers, the plots often revolve around two star-crossed lovers who must overcome countless obstacles to be united in the end. It is not uncommon for an

Indian to see the same movie fifteen times over the duration of its theatrical release.

In the 1980s, pirated videocassettes were seen as a threat to the film industry, but the mafia soon took control of that outlet as well. At the time, most of the filmgoers in India were male, and there was an abundance of action, disco, and rape-revenge movies in release. By the end of the decade, however, teen romance had taken hold of audiences as changes in demographics had more young people, especially females, coming to theaters. Budgets began to rise as ever more sophisticated moviegoers were influenced by American movies, readily available in India on videotape, and they demanded the biggest stars, the most spectacular settings, the best music, which pressured producers to raise even more money. As a change of pace, films now were being shot in the United States, England, and Scotland to placate audiences who grew bored with the same old Indian scenic backdrops appearing in film after film.

Throughout the decade, Dawood tapped further into the thriving Bollywood film industry, bullying stars and producers, and eventually financing many films himself.

Abu Salem, a.k.a. Abdul Saleem Ansari, was a taxi driver in Delhi when he decided to make the move to Bombay in the 1980s. He managed to find work as a small-timer in Dawood Ibrahim's D

Company, engaging in petty crime and operating a telephone booth in Andheri, a northern suburb of Bombay. It wasn't long before Salem managed to prove himself to higher-ups in D Company, and he was promoted to Dawood's gunrunner. His job was a simple one but one he delivered on time and again: He was in charge of moving D Company's arsenal from point to point in Bombay for use by Ibrahim's hit men and sharpshooters, and Salem made the most of his relationships with the *bhais* (brothers) of D Company. One of those bhais was actually Dawood's younger brother, Anees.

Salem quickly gained enough confidence to begin extorting money from real estate developers around the city, but there was an industry in Bombay that the former taxi driver from the Azamgarh district of Uttar Pradesh had long dreamed of being a part of. Eventually, Salem rose within D Company's ranks to second lieutenant, and he was determined to make his mark in Bollywood. But he was not interested in financing films. Instead, he carved out his own niche through extortion and buying out the rights to films, often through intimidation or worse. So violent and deadly were the bhais of D Company that Salem's conversations with producers rarely had to go beyond a friendly "chat" to get the message across. A new leading lady needed to be put in a given movie immediately, perhaps, or an unexpected payment suddenly came due. For years, producers and stars lived in fear of their phones ringing with offers they couldn't refuse. Too often, the caller on the other end was Salem.

Over the years, Salem's success controlling the extortion racket in Bollywood enabled him to rise to second in command of D Company. Then, in 1997, in a failed extortion bid, producer and music baron Gulshan Kumar was gunned down in broad daylight. Abu Salem was believed responsible. A few months later, Salem was charged with attempted murder of another famous Bollywood producer, Rajiv Rai. Later still, it was learned that Salem was behind the killing of Ajit Deewani, the secretary of movie actress Manisha Koirala. Deewani had been shot dead outside his office, presumably for not carrying out Salem's "suggestions." At a time when the industry was struggling financially, this brazenness sent waves of fear rippling through the community. Yet Dawood's bhais were getting rich beyond their wildest dreams.

Despite evidence that Salem was involved in the Bombay serial blasts, he managed to maintain control of Bollywood for Dawood, even though he wasn't actually in India himself. Operating out of Kenya, South Africa, and Dubai, Salem had a famous falling out in 1998 with Chhota Shakeel, another of Dawood's most trusted aides, when Shakeel tried to muscle in on Salem's territory. The split triggered a vicious power struggle for the glitzy, lucrative Bollywood film industry, but Salem's luck was about to run out. In 2002, the former taxi driver and

Dawood gunrunner was arrested and detained in Lisbon, Portugal, where he still is awaiting extradition to India.

Much has changed in Bollywood since Salem's capture. The government of India has attempted to clean up the industry by allowing banks to finance movies, cutting down on the need for the type of private financing that led to so much corruption. Police also have begun to crack down on the influence of the mafia. That said, corruption within the Indian film industry seems endemic, and no one expects changes overnight. Reports suggest that the mafia may be funding fewer movies today, instead moving on to gain control of the distribution of films worldwide while continuing to influence the films themselves by "placing" bankable stars in those films they have the most interest in profiting from.

Dawood Ibrahim, however, has risen above petty extortion and funding schemes in Bollywood. Still, he continues to maintain a nostalgic interest in the industry that reminds him so much of a homeland he can never return to. In Dubai, Ibrahim would host lavish parties where he would fly in his favorite stars and put deals together that would earn him millions. It was at one of these parties that Dawood met Mandakini, the beautiful star of *Ram Teri Ganga Maili*, with whom he had a child that he supports to this day.

Ironically, Ibrahim was the subject of a film himself, *Company*, directed by Ram Gopal Verma, who is sometimes referred to as the "Martin Scorsese of Bollywood." Verma reportedly endured some sleepless nights while trying to decide on an ending to his "underworld" film. He chose two big stars: Ajay Devgan played Dawood and Vivek Oberoi played Dawood's bitter rival, Chhota Rajan. Verma was more than a little concerned that neither mobster would appreciate seeing his celluloid self shot down, and might even express displeasure. It was rumored that Verma shot separate endings with each don gunned down—something he later denied. This *Godfather*-like epic was a big hit in India, and Verma ultimately settled on a climax that was somewhat ambiguous. Still, it is likely that neither Dawood Ibrahim nor Chhota Rajan was pleased with the way the movie ended.

"Our idea was to capture him [Chhota Rajan] alive and bring him to Dubai. But he jumped out of his window and tried to escape, so we had to shoot him. We had not planned to kill him so easily."

–Chhota Shakeel

CHAPTER FOUR

MAFIA WARS:
A DEADLY SPLIT WITHIN D COMPANY

The true-to-life story of the feud between Dawood Ibrahim and his former associate, Chhota Rajan, is a bloody saga that seems to spring right from the pages of a Quentin Tarantino script. After the Bombay blasts in '93, D Company began to splinter—most notably, along the lines of Hindus and Muslims. Rajan, a Hindi, was one of Dawood's top lieutenants and Dawood considered him one of his "nine jewels." When Rajan defected, he formed his own group, made up mostly of Hindus, and it is widely believed that India's external intelligence outfit, the Research and Analysis Wing (RAW), began to cultivate Rajan against Dawood, even offering him financial support to mobilize.

Chhota Rajan grew up as Rajan Nikhalje on the streets of Tilak Nagar, Chembur, a suburb in central Bombay. Though his early life was nowhere near as desperate as Dawood Ibrahim's, like his future boss Rajan learned early on that a life of crime might be his only path to power, money, and respect. And like many aspiring gangsters, he was eager to prove himself in the extortion rackets and the sale of film tickets on the black market. He finally gained the favor of Varadaragan Mudaliar, and together they began expanding their small enterprise to include smuggling. As they grew, Rajan forged a relationship with a powerful Bombay mafiosa don named Baba Rajan, who mentored the young Chhota Rajan until a rival, Qunju, had Baba Rajan killed. Qunju was a very powerful man in Bombay, and the killing devastated Chhota Rajan. When Rajan learned of Qunju's passion for cricket, he hatched a plot to avenge the murder.

During a cricket match in which Qunju was playing, three young, ragged-looking boys who had been watching the match stepped into the arena, presumably to help retrieve the ball for Qunju. Instead, they pulled guns from their jerseys and shot Qunju dead, in full view of spectators. Before long, everyone knew that Rajan Nikhalje was behind the killing, and he was dubbed "Chhota Rajan" in honor of Baba Rajan.

This bold killing helped catch the eye of the higher-ups in D Company, and Rajan was taken under the wing of Dawood Ibrahim. What followed was a spectacular rise in the fortunes of D Company as Chhota Rajan became one of Dawood's most powerful and deadly lieutenants—qualities that, much later, would come back to haunt Dawood. In 1984, when Dawood fled India for Dubai, he left Rajan in charge of his Bombay operations, where Rajan cultivated his own relationships in Dawood's absence. But soon, according to writer S. Hussain Zaidi, Rajan was forced to leave Bombay as well, and the two teamed up again in Dubai until the late 1980s.

After the Bombay serial blasts, it was believed that the Hindu members of D Company were no longer willing to work under the control of Dawood Ibrahim, a Muslim. (However, many Hindus continued working in D Company, and it has been pointed out that Rajan did not leave Dawood immediately following the blasts.) Rajan did take several key Hindu figures in D Company with him, and their departure sparked one of the most notorious and bloodiest gang wars in the history of Bombay. Several of Chhota Rajan's hit men were dispatched to Dubai to assassinate Sunil "Sawtya" Sawant, one of the few remaining Hindu supporters of Dawood and a key leader in D Company. Dawood immediately retaliated, setting off a chain reaction of violence. Rajan countered by killing several more of Dawood's top aides. In all, gang warfare claimed the lives of fifty-two men in 1996, the majority with some connection to the bitter rivalry between the two D Company leaders.

By 1998, Rajan had escalated the war by targeting ISI operatives and those with connections to Dawood Ibrahim who were responsible for the Bombay blasts. These systematic executions were something of a public relations move on the part of Rajan, who made an effort to portray himself as the "patriotic don" after his split with Dawood. Then, Mirza Dilshad Beg, a Nepalese politician who was believed to be providing safe houses and other assistance to the ISI, was gunned down by Chhota Rajan's men on June 29, 1998.

The split after the Bombay blasts also led to an alliance between Rajan and other mafia leaders in South Asia, such as Uttar Pradesh's Om Prakash "Babloo" Srivastava. All this had a significant effect on Dawood's empire, as there were signs D Company was in chaos. Dawood's brother, Anees, made an attempt at establishing himself as a D Company heavyweight by ordering the assassinations of key Dawood confidents in Bombay. Police in the city were content to let these mafia battles play out rather than try to stem the violence. However, Dawood was simply biding his time, waiting to launch an offensive that would escalate the violence even further.

During the summer of 2000, Dawood Ibrahim put several teams of assassins to the task of locating and killing his once trusted aide and now bitter rival, Chhota Rajan. The assassins were stationed in Malaysia, Australia, Dubai, India, and Thailand. Ultimately, through an informer, Rohit Verma, also one of Rajan's deadliest hit men, the assassins were able to track the former D Company lieutenant to Bangkok, where they patiently stalked their target for months. On September 15, Verma tipped off D Company, and the seven to ten assassins, dressed in black suits, white shirts, and black ties, approached the security gate of the apartment complex where Rajan was staying. It is alleged that they arrived with a birthday cake, claiming it was in honor of Rajan, and were granted entry, although some reports suggest the security guard may have been overpowered. What is known is that six people were killed in the subsequent hail of gunfire.

D Company had reason to celebrate. The following day, headlines around the world announced the death of Chhota Rajan, the mafia don who dared to stand up to Dawood Ibrahim. But the party was short-lived. Rajan was actually the lone survivor of the attack, and he was in intensive care in a Bangkok hospital, surrounded by around-the-clock police protection.

Asia Times correspondent Sheela Bhatt managed to land an interview with Dawood lieutenant Chhota Shakeel on the evening of September 15. The interview was remarkable in how beyond candid Shakeel was about his team of assassins in Bangkok. Even more remarkable, at the time of the interview Shakeel was under the impression that Rajan was dead.

"Our idea was to capture him alive and bring him to Dubai," Shakeel told Bhatt. "But he jumped out of his window and tried to escape, so we had to shoot him. We had not planned to kill him so easily."

Chhota Shakeel went on to tell Bhatt that "The entire D Gang is behind this," and supplied the reporter with specific information about the planning of the operation, including the number of assassins and how they were able to track Rajan to Bangkok. When Bhatt specifically asked why D Company was so upset with Rajan, Shakeel became incredulous. "He ran away from Dubai with crores of rupees' worth of gold belonging to us," Shakeel said. "He was willing to do anything for money. You should know more. Don't you read the newspapers in Bombay? Don't you know how many murders are against him in Bombay?"

Initial reports of Chhota Rajan's death were only the first of numerous inaccurate and mysterious reports coming out of Bangkok in the weeks following the failed assassination attempt. On September 17, the *Tribune* in Chandigarh, India, had Rajan alive and recovering but moved to Malaysia for security reasons. In fact, Rajan remained in the intensive care unit of Samitivej Hospital in Bangkok, still in critical condition. Ultimately, the victims of the shootout would total six: Rajan's informer, Rohit Verma; Verma's wife, Sarita; and their two-year-old daughter, as well as the watchman at Rajan's apartment, a bodyguard, and another associate of Rajan's.

On September 28, Rajan was wheeled into a Bangkok courtroom on a stretcher, with oxygen and intravenous bags suspended above him, to answer the false passport charges that were filed against him. There, Rajan made the following statement to Thai authorities regarding the attack on his life two weeks before:

I was calling to Thailand by my friend Michael [Rohit Verma]. On September 15, 2000 at 9:45 pm I was shot twice. One bullet in the stomach and one near the kidney.

I was in my house. I was locking the door. Bullets hit the door. At the time of the incident, Michael, his wife, his child, and one maidservant were present in the flat. Except for the maidservant, all of us were Indians. I was not aware where they were in the flat.

I was sleeping in my room when I heard the sound of firing, which woke me up. From the sound I came to know that there was firing going on in the hall. A number of bullets were fired. I was standing near the door when the two bullets hit me.

I tried to lock the door. When the bullets cracked the door and hit me, I came to know about the number of bullets that were fired at me. I am not exactly sure then, but I thought two bullets him me. The door is made of plywood.

My window was shut. When the bullet sounds stopped and it was quiet I opened it by force. The flat is on the first floor. There is a wall near the window. With the help of the wall I came down to the ground. Near the wall there was a garbage box. It was full. I covered myself with the garbage and hid inside.

It was dark around that corner, but I was able to see the passers-by.

Nobody could see me. I was safe in the garbage box. I did not hear any sound of firing or anybody's voice. I remained under the filth for 10 minutes. Then I went to the basement and up to my flat.

I saw some people standing outside. The door was open. I went inside. I saw Michael and his wife lying on the floor. Somebody had taken the child away. I did not know which weapon was used to shoot at me. Then the police came.

I am not aware of which hospital I was admitted to. I and bhabbi [Rohit's wife] are being treated in the same hospital. In Thailand and in India, I have no enemy. I am not aware who they were and why they were trying to kill me. There have been no attempts on my life ever and I do not know the shooters. I do not know anybody among them.

But the episode was far from over. For ten weeks, Bombay police waited anxiously for the call from New Delhi to come ordering them to fly to Bangkok and bring Rajan back to India to face numerous criminal charges, including multiple counts of murder. Yet on November 24, Bangkok newspapers were reporting that Chhota Rajan had escaped from Samitivej Hospital by tying some bedsheets together and shinnying down from the fourth floor of the hospital. Once he reached the ground, he was hurried to a waiting boat that took him to the airport, where he had his private jet waiting.

"I am in Europe," Rajan exclaimed in an interview from an undisclosed location. The "escape" was a considerable embarrassment to Bangkok police, who had assured India that

Rajan was being held under the most stringent security measures. Initial reports suggested that he had somehow drugged his guards. "I took hardly two minutes to escape and the poor guards did not know about it," he told the *Star News*.

The escape was also an embarrassment to Indian authorities, who appeared to have dragged their heels while preparing extradition papers when Rajan was completely vulnerable to arrest. But the embarrassment in New Delhi was soon replaced by scandal in Bangkok as it was soon learned that Rajan's escape had less to do with sheets and drugs and more to do with bribery. According to a story by Bertil Lintner, Sirichai Piyaphichetkul, Rajan's lawyer in Bangkok, stated that Rajan simply handed over twenty-five million *baht* ($580,000) to Kriekphong Phukprayoon, the Thai police major general (Phukprayoon denied it). The payoff enabled a much less dramatic escape. Rajan simply walked out to the hospital parking lot, got in a car, and drove away.

Rajan's escape led to the firing of nine Bangkok police officials for "grave negligence." But it only temporarily distracted Indians from negligence in their own country of far greater concern. Why did it take so long for New Delhi to act on the extradition of one of India's most notorious criminals? Skeptics are convinced that there was never any intention to bring Rajan back to India, that the government simply was biding its time until the mafia don could escape. But why? Chhota Shakeel, in an interview with Sheela Raval after he learned of Rajan's escape, hinted at what could be the true reason Rajan was never extradited to India to face charges. Because he had aligned himself with Indian intelligence agencies against Muslim extremists and Pakistan's ISI, Rajan somehow was considered a national hero in India. According to Shakeel, Rajan is "supported by Indian authorities and protected by Indian authorities."

Shakeel told Raval: "We have to eliminate Rajan anyhow because he is not just a traitor but is trying to become a patriot...Tell me what he has done for India. He is just another gangster like us."

Aside from denying Dawood's involvement with the ISI and the terrorist group LeT (Lashkar-e-Toiba), Shakeel also mocked Rajan in the Raval interview: "He was lucky but a coward. Instead of facing bullets like a good warrior, he showed his back and ran away. Anyway, better luck next time. My man, Munna Jingada (alias Mohammed Saleem), who is in police custody now, is a capable man and he won't miss a second chance."

Some in India continue to point to Rajan as a champion of the people's interests, solely because of his willingness to use his resources to counter the ISI. It is believed by some that the ISI provided Chhota Shakeel with global positioning systems and other high tech imaging to help track Rajan to Thailand. If true, it would only confirm what many suspect—Pakistani and

Indian agencies are using respective mafia gangs to gain strategic intelligence and espionage advantages over each other.

After denying the former Bombay

mobster was ever in the country,

Pakistan has reversed course and

stated unequivocally that it will not

turn him over to India.

CHAPTER FIVE

DAWOOD IBRAHIM
AND PAKISTAN'S ISI:
WARNING SIGNS OF TERROR

Dawood Ibrahim has been living under the protection of Pakistan's Inter-Services Intelligence (ISI) since 1994. Moving between Karachi and Islamabad under heavy guard at all times, he maintains a complex relationship with the ISI. According to some estimates, he provides the ISI with $1 billion each year, and gives the agency access to hit men from his terrorist group Lashkar-e-Toiba (LeT)—which is considered "the sword of the ISI." Perhaps of most value to the ISI has been Dawood's willingness to support intelligence efforts against India. Since he organized the Bombay blasts in 1993, Dawood has been India's public enemy number one, and by cooperating with the ISI in areas of espionage and continued terrorism against Indian interests he has solidified his allegiance to Pakistan. In fact, after denying the former Bombay mobster was ever in the country, Pakistan has reversed course and stated unequivocally that it will not turn him over to India.

"Shortly after Ibrahim left Dubai for Karachi in the wake of the Mumbai [Bombay] serial bombings, he was issued a passport back-dated to August 12, 1991, bearing the number G-866537, in Rawalpindi. Soon afterwards, he moved into a 6,000-sq m plot in the upmarket Clifton area of Karachi that had amenities such as a swimming pool, gymnasium and tennis court," reported Praveen Swami, for *Frontline*, one of India's premiere magazines. Swami also reported that Shakeel was rewarded with just as palatial a residence in the Defence Housing Authority enclave, while Memon, the other accomplice in the Bombay blasts, rewarded himself by buying two or three lavish homes, "including the multi-storey Kashif Crown plaza situated on the Shara-e-Faisal boulevard."

According to Swami, all of D Company's higher-ups received more than ample security to guard them just in case Indian intelligence or Ibrahim's underworld archenemies decided to make any attempts on his or their lives. "Two bullet-proof cars were at his disposal round the clock, and a 12-member official guard was placed at his Clifton residence." Dawood, as Hasnain reported in the Pakistani newspaper *Newsline*, invariably woke up past noon, and, after a game of tennis or snooker, set off "for any of his safehouses in Karachi for an evening of revelry—usually comprising drinks (he prefers a certain 'Black Label' brand), mujras (performances by female dancers) and gambling. Carousing through the night, Dawood and his companions quit only at dawn and then collectively offer prayers. This has been his routine for years."

When Dawood Ibrahim and company moved into their posh digs, local residents attempted to protest in print to the government, but the ISI immediately closed any protests down and told local residents that the buildings were owned by Dawood, a legitimate citizen in the country's eyes, and to be quiet. Few Pakistanis are willing to take on the ISI.

It has been noted that the ISI now holds a great deal of power over Dawood Ibrahim, however, especially after he was declared a global terrorist by the U.S. State Department in the fall of 2003. Intense pressure to crack down on global terrorism has, in effect, made it impossible for him to leave Pakistan. One of the few safe havens left in the world for Dawood and his D Company had been Dubai, where he had stayed frequently even before his implication in the Bombay blasts. But the United Arab Emirates recently signed an extradition treaty with India and has been attempting to shed its image as a breeding ground for gangsters and Islamic extremists by cooperating in the war against terror. It is believed that Dawood is not only not welcome in Dubai anymore but would face extradition to India should he enter the country. So while Dawood may be living his life as the King of Karachi under ISI protection, and despite his billions and his own personal army, he is also keenly aware that his survival is somewhat contingent on his usefulness to the ISI. To this day, he continues to be extraordinarily useful to Pakistani intelligence.

One might wonder just how a crime lord and terrorist such as Dawood Ibrahim could be permitted to conduct business as usual in a country that has sworn its allegiance to the United States in the war against terror, especially after the events of 9/11. To understand this permissiveness, it is important to understand the history of Pakistan's Inter-Services Intelligence agency. The Center for Cooperative Research has been instrumental in compiling information relating to the events of September 11, and has cited numerous reports, mainstream as well as independent, on the activities of Pakistan's ISI over the years, many of which are presented here. Following is a brief history of the ISI, mainly focusing on the events that helped define Pakistan as it exists today—namely, the effect of the Soviet invasion of Afghanistan. It is essential in understanding how Dawood Ibrahim can survive and prosper. In the larger sense, the world is still dealing with the consequences and fallout of the United States and Saudi Arabia having poured vast amounts of money and weapons into Afghanistan to fight the Soviet Union.

Pakistan's Inter-Services Intelligence was founded in 1948 by Major General R. Cawthorne, a British Army officer who was then the deputy chief of staff in the Pakistan Army. By the 1950s, Field Marshal Ayub Khan, the president of Pakistan, decided to expand the role of the ISI with the goal of safeguarding Pakistan's interests, keeping the military in charge of the country, and spying on politicians. In 1970, however, Zulfiqar Ali Bhutto, who openly criticized the ISI in the general elections, was instrumental in diminishing the importance of the agency in the years he held power in Pakistan. But it was not long before the ISI regained its importance. In 1977, with the help of the ISI, General Muhammad Zia ul-Haq seized power, and just two years later the Soviet Union staged an act of aggression that helped cement the influence of the ISI in Pakistan to this day.

On December 26, 1979, the Soviets invaded Afghanistan, and what followed was a complex web of covert actions involving, among countless others, the CIA, Pakistan's Inter-Services Intelligence, and Prince Turki al-Faisal, the head of Saudi Arabia's secret service. Tensions between the United States and Russia were at the highest level since the Vietnam War, perhaps even since the Cuban missile crisis, and the United States was determined to do everything short of sending troops to the region to counter what was perceived around the world as an unprovoked act of aggression on the part of the Russians. The Saudis were none too thrilled with the prospect of the communist superpower creeping into their oil-rich backyard, and, like the U.S., they were willing to contribute large sums of money toward ousting the Soviets from Afghanistan. It is believed that the Saudis matched the U.S. dollar for dollar for the length of the war, and some estimates put the total figure at $40 billion.

Pakistan was in no position to fund the war, but thousands of the country's Muslims were willing to fight and die defending their fellow Muslims in neighboring Afghanistan. Before long, money and sophisticated weaponry were flowing into Pakistan to be funneled to the *mujahedeen* guerrillas, a dedicated army comprised mostly of Afghanis and Pakistanis. And the overwhelming portion of these resources were managed by the ISI.

In the early stages of the Afghan war, as more and more money from the United States and Saudi Arabia poured into the region, opium production in Afghanistan began to explode. Alfred McCoy, professor of Southeast Asian Studies at the University of Wisconsin, stated that U.S. and Pakistani intelligence were willing to tolerate the rebels' drug trafficking because of their deep hatred of the Russians. "If their local allies were involved in narcotics trafficking, it didn't trouble the CIA. They were willing to keep working with people who were heavily involved in narcotics."

It is believed that Afghan opium production increased from 250 to 2,000 tons per year over the course of the ten-year war, under the direction of the ISI. As early as 1980, Osama bin Laden began funding the mujahedeen in Afghanistan with millions from his family's fortune, as well as helping to engineer the resistance against the Soviets. There is some speculation that bin Laden was appointed for this task by Saudi prince Turki himself. By 1984, bin Laden left Saudi Arabia for Peshawar, a Pakistani town on the Afghan border, where he established a front organization called Maktab al-Khidamar (MAK), which funneled funds, arms, and soldiers directly into the war. The ISI and the CIA found bin Laden tremendously useful in the fight against the Soviets, and it was through MAK that he met Gulbuddin Hekmatyar, the notorious rebel leader who had acquired a significant number of the CIA's covert weapons. Hekmatyar's ability to stealthily negotiate the mountains in Afghanistan not only strengthened the mujahedeen resistance, it enabled him to set up and secure major drug trafficking routes that exist to this day.

By the mid 1980s, with the war against the Soviets at full pitch, the ISI (under CIA direction) developed a secret cell of agents who used the profits from heroin production to fund covert activities. Their number one priority was to turn Russian soldiers into heroin addicts and they met with some success. Afghanistan was becoming something of a Vietnam for the Soviet Union; the soldiers no longer understood why they were there, and the prospect of fighting "ghosts" in the cold and desolate mountains was having a detrimental effect on their psyche. The abundance of heroin in the region proved to be a temptation many soldiers could not resist in their attempts to survive a combination of monotony and sporadic terror. And the mujahedeen warriors "spooked" the Russians for several reasons. Absolutely fearless and dedicated to their cause, their lifeless eyes and ability to withstand pain was nothing the Soviets had ever encountered. In fact, the Russians had expected to overwhelm the Afghans with little resistance. But that resistance seemed to grow as the years of occupation passed. The mujahedeen, knowing they could not beat the Russians with firepower, demoralized their aggressors psychologically: Small teams would creep into Russian camps and abduct one or two men. Sometimes the soldiers would be tortured, mutilated, then left for their comrades to discover at daybreak; others would be forced to be mujahedeen "concubines" for weeks at a time, then returned broken, desolated, and scarred for life. Many soldiers felt it better to kill themselves rather than risk capture, so it was no surprise that there was such a market for heroin among the Russian ranks.

The ISI also knew there was a healthy demand for heroin outside the military, and, with all the money coming in to develop weapons for the mujahedeen, the drug refineries and smuggling routes along the Afghan/Pakistani border thrived. Money made from smuggling drugs to Western countries actually supplemented the Pakistani economy. "But for these heroin dollars, Pakistan's legitimate economy must have collapsed many years ago."

And since these vast sums of money were coming into the Pakistani economy through the ISI, it was only natural that the ISI became an autonomous power, or Pakistan's "invisible government." By the spring of 1985, the United States began to escalate the war in Afghanistan by mounting guerrilla attacks into Tajikistan and Uzbekistan, at that time Soviet territories. The attacks targeted the military and factories, but, more important, the CIA began working with the ISI to aggressively recruit radical Muslims from around the world to fight the Soviets. Armed with subversive literature and the Koran, the ISI was able to bring in more than thirty thousand Muslim radicals from over forty countries, including the Soviet Union itself.

In Pakistan, tens of thousands were studying in hundreds of new *madrassas*, schools of radical Islam teachings that were funded by the ISI and the CIA. The mujahedeen network grew exponentially, causing then Pakistani president Benazir Bhutto to warn President George H. W. Bush, "You are creating a Frankenstein." But the CIA was beginning to sense a turning of the tide in the fight against the Soviets, and Bhutto's warning did not resonate. After the Afghanistan war, thousands of mujahedeen would return to Peshawar and engage in countless acts of terrorism, forcing the president of Pakistan to ask the military for help in regaining control of the city. One Western diplomat noted that these returning mujahedeen would never have been trained or united without the help of the United States. "The consequences for all of us are astronomical."

With money flowing in from the CIA and the ISI, and with the help of Osama bin Laden, the mujahedeen began constructing the Khost tunnel complex in Afghanistan, which was instrumental in fighting the Soviets. (These same tunnels later would become targets when the United States was ousting the Taliban from power in 2001.) Soviet troops withdrew from Afghanistan in 1988, and it was around this time that bin Laden formed al-Qaeda.

It is believed that bin Laden broke ties with the CIA after the first Gulf War ended in 1991, when thousands of U.S. soldiers become stationed permanently in Saudi Arabia, his former home. He released a statement in 1998 stating, "For more than seven years the United States has been occupying the lands of Islam in the holiest of places, the Arabian peninsula, plundering its riches, dictating to its rulers, humiliating its people, terrorizing its neighbors, and turning its bases in the peninsula into a spearhead through which to fight the neighboring Muslim peoples." It was around this time that al-Qaeda began targeting U.S. interests, and the Western world began to recognize the prophetic warning of Benazir Bhutto.

In 1991, the Bank of England shut down the Bank of Credit and Commerce International (BCCI), based in Pakistan and the largest Muslim bank in the world. BCCI was financing countless Muslim terrorist organizations and engaged in money laundering for illicit activities such as drug trafficking and arms dealing. "BCCI did dirty work for every major terrorist service in the world," reported the *Los Angeles Times*.

Not surprisingly, the ISI was doing a great deal of business with the BCCI, and both the British and U.S. governments were aware of these dealings. The CIA had been using the BCCI to funnel millions of dollars to the mujahedeen, and this effort was so successful in driving communism out of Afghanistan that the agency was willing to overlook what they deemed at the time to be the lesser of two evils. Yet around the world, the repercussions of a well-financed radical Islam force were beginning to make ripples, if not waves.

In late October of 2001, <u>The Economist</u> reported that the Taliban were dumping their stockpile of heroin into the market to pay for the war against the U.S. There is little chance of this happening without the consent of Dawood Ibrahim and D Company.

CHAPTER SIX

THE PATH TO 9/11: OSAMA BIN LADEN AND DAWOOD IBRAHIM

Khalid Shaikh Mohammad would later become known as the mastermind behind the September 11 attacks in New York and Washington, D.C., but as far back as the early 1990s he was arousing suspicion internationally because of his connections to terrorist activities in the Philippines and his access to large sums of money. After the World Trade Center bombing in 1993, he lived in the Philippines, where he planned the Bojinka plot, an audacious plan to simultaneously destroy twelve airliners over the Pacific Ocean and fly a suicide bomber into CIA headquarters in Langley, Virginia. The supposedly devout Muslim led a lavish and decadent lifestyle there, counting go-go dancers as girlfriends and throwing expensive "big drinking" parties in four-star hotels. He took scuba lessons, and he even rented a helicopter at one point just to fly by the house of a girlfriend who he was trying to impress. It is believed that Shaikh Mohammad was backed by ISI money while in the Philippines, and there is speculation that he may have met with some of the 9/11 hijackers there. What is known is that he was nearly captured there in 1999 while visiting yet another girlfriend, and he was directly involved in a failed plot to assassinate the Pope. Evidence would later be uncovered implicating Shaikh Mohammad in the 1998 U.S. Embassy bombings in Kenya and Tanzania, and the 2000 USS *Cole* bombing. According to one U.S. official, "There is a clear operational link between him and the execution of most, if not all, of the al-Qaeda plots over the past five years." The United States went so far as to offer a $2 million reward for his capture in 1998, and some reports indicated that he may even have been an ISI agent at the time.

Another key figure emerged around the same time as Shaikh Mohammad, though from an entirely different background. Sometime in June 1993, a brilliant British student at the London School of Economics was having second thoughts about a career in finance. Saeed Ahmed Sheikh dropped out of the prestigious school and moved to Pakistan, where his intelligence was most appreciated by the hard-core fundamentalists he swore allegiance to. He trained in Afghanistan at al-Qaeda camps run by the Pakistani Army, and the following year he became an instructor himself. His specialty was the kidnapping of Western tourists in India, but it was a short-lived career since he was captured in October 1994 and imprisoned. It was later learned that the ISI hired Sheikh's defense lawyer, but he was held nonetheless for five years without a trial in a maximum security prison.

It was in prison that Saeed Sheikh met Aftab Ansari, an Indian gangster, and Asif Raza Khan, whom, after his release from prison in 1999, he would begin working with in the kidnappings of Indians. Some of the profits from these kidnappings would later be linked to the funding of 9/11. It was around this time that Sheikh also began working with another associate he met in prison, Maulana Masood Azhar, a known terrorist with al-Qaeda and ISI connections. In late December 1999, with Sheikh still serving his prison term, members of *Harkat-ul-Mujahdeen*, another group of terrorists organized by Azhar, hijacked an Indian Airlines flight to Afghanistan and held 155 passengers hostage for over a week. The terrorists killed an Indian businessman, then demanded the release of Azhar, Sheikh, and another militant being held in an Indian prison. Eventually, India met their demands and released the three militants. Azhar surfaced in Pakistan a few days later and addressed a thong of some ten thousand supporters, proclaiming, "I have come here because this is my duty to tell you that Muslims should not rest in peace until we have destroyed America and India." Under the protection of the ISI, Azhar toured Pakistan, and, together with Sheikh, formed the terrorist group *Jaish-e-Mohammad*, under the watchful guidance of the ISI. Freed from prison, Sheikh stayed in Kandahar, Afghanistan, and met with the leader of the Taliban, Mullah Omar. He also met with Osama bin Laden, who referred to Sheikh as "my special son." It is interesting to note that at the same time these notorious relationships were being cemented the United States was giving $113 million in humanitarian aid to the Taliban, according to the State Department. Sheikh traveled to Pakistan, meanwhile, and is believed to have been given a house by the ISI. Because he was able to help al-Qaeda establish an "encrypted Web-based communication system," he was considered a valuable asset to the ISI. There was even talk of him as an eventual successor to bin Laden. He was working alongside Lieutenant General Mohammad Aziz Khan, former deputy chief of the ISI in charge of relations with Jaish-e-Mohammad, and Brigadier Abdullah, a former ISI officer who was making frequent trips to Afghanistan for the training of new recruits. It was around this time that Sheikh is believed to have helped train the September 11 hijackers.

It is worth noting that U.S. intelligence was not completely in the dark about the dangers presented by Dawood Ibrahim and the ISI even before the September 11 wake-up call.

According to a story in the *New York Times*, when President Clinton visited Pakistan on March 25, 2000, the Secret Service believed the ISI was so thoroughly infiltrated by terrorist organizations that it begged the president to cancel the visit. Clinton insisted on going, however, and his security went to such extraordinary and unprecedented precautions as to fly the empty Air Force One into Pakistan while the president landed in a small, unmarked plane.

By September 1994, Afghani exiles living in Pakistan began to take control of Afghanistan. The Taliban, as they became known, quickly swept into power, and experts at the time explained that their overwhelming military success was a sure sign that the ISI was behind them. In fact, a regional source with extensive ties to the CIA was quoted as saying, "I warned them that we were creating a monster." Later he would say, "The Taliban are not just recruits from 'madrassas' but are on the payroll of the ISI."

In November 2001, the *Wall Street Journal* stated, "Despite their clean chins and pressed uniforms, the ISI men are as deeply fundamentalist as any bearded fanatic; the ISI created the Taliban as their own instrument and still supports it."

In 1996, Arian Airlines was the national airline of Afghanistan. It may have been the quirkiest airline in the world, as any passenger would attest. Scheduled flights became fewer and fewer, and dependability became something of a crapshoot. But Arian was not having a cash problem. The reason? Al-Qaeda had assumed control, turning the airline into the transportation of choice for its illegal drug, weapons, and gold trade between Afghanistan, Pakistan, and the United Arab Emirates.

As many as four flights a day were running these routes. The Afghans taxed the opium production, which was paid in gold bullion, and then the bullion was flown to Dubai and laundered into cash. At the time, U.S. intelligence was aware of the Ariana smuggling flights and attempted to press the UAE to enforce stricter banking controls. But "not wanting to offend an ally in an already complicated relationship," they were wary of creating more tension in the region. By 1999, the United Nations had imposed sanctions against Afghanistan because of Ariana's illegal activities, but the sanctions did little to slow the airline. It wasn't until October 2001, when the U.S. began to bomb Afghanistan, that Ariana finally was drummed out of business. Later, reports would suggest that the airline may even have had a role in training the 9/11 suicide pilots.

With Dawood Ibrahim's D Company firmly entrenched in Dubai's money laundering networks, it's no stretch to assume that he was making use of Ariana's carrier services, either directly or indirectly. Ibrahim no doubt also encountered the mysterious Victor Bout, a.k.a. "the Merchant of Death," in the fall of 1996. Bout, a Russian arms merchant, had been selling weapons to Afghanistan's Northern Alliance since 1992. However, in October 1996, he had a financially motivated change of heart and began selling his highly sought after weapons to the Taliban and al-Qaeda. He delivered at least forty tons of Soviet-made weapons to the Taliban that year, taking in over $50 million. According to intelligence, it is believed that he was able to conduct his dealings with the Taliban "on behalf of the Pakistan government." A few years later, the ISI cut a deal with Bout, bringing nearly two hundred T-55 and T-62 tanks from the Ukrainians into Afghanistan.

Viktor Bout may have shared something else with Osama bin Laden besides a willingness to work with the Taliban. Like bin Laden, the Merchant of Death was believed to have been working with the CIA. However, Bout was suspected of helping the CIA arm Afghanistan's Northern Alliance at a time when bin Laden was clearly in the Taliban camp.

By late 1996, bin Laden had established a major role in the drug smuggling trade. The profits realized from opium funded the Taliban as well as his own terror network. Yoseff Bodansky, director of the congressional Task Force on Terrorism and Unconventional Warfare, reported that bin Laden was taking up to a 15 percent cut of drug money in exchange for the protection of smugglers and the laundering of their profits. If accurate, this would put bin Laden's share at approximately $1 billion, given the estimates of Afghanistan's drug profits ($6.5 billion to $10 billion) each year. Regardless of the exact percentage of bin Laden's cut, it pales in comparison to the amount Dawood Ibrahim is taking from the region. After September 11, bin Laden is believed to have come to a financial agreement with Ibrahim to use the King of Karachi's drug smuggling routes in Pakistan and Afghanistan to avoid capture by U.S. forces.

In retaliation for the U.S. Embassy bombings, the United States fired sixty-six cruise missiles at suspected al-Qaeda training camps in Afghanistan, and thirteen more at a pharmaceutical factory in Khartoum, Sudan. The missiles killed more than thirty people, but none were believed to be major al-Qaeda targets. After the bombing, President Clinton claimed the missiles were aimed at a "gathering of key terrorist leaders," but it turned out that the supposed gathering occurred a month earlier in Pakistan. However, included among the dead in the suspected al-Qaeda camps were five ISI officers and twenty trainees.

The failed attack on Osama bin Laden raised his stature in the Muslim world. A U.S. defense analyst said, "I think that raid really helped elevate bin Laden's reputation in a big way, building him up in the Muslim world. . . . My sense is that because the attack was so limited and incompetent, we turned this guy into a folk hero."

On March 7, 2001, the Russian Permanent Mission at the

United Nations submitted a top secret and "unprecedentedly detailed report" to the UN Security Council about Osama bin Laden. Included in the report was information about bin Laden's whereabouts, the inner command structure and workings of the al-Qaeda network, Afghan drug running, and Taliban connections in Pakistan. The report also includes "a listing of all bin Laden's bases, his government contacts and foreign advisors." Alex Standish, the editor of *Jane's Intelligence Review*, would later come to the conclusion that the attacks of 9/11 were less indicative of an American failure in intelligence and more the result of "a political decision not to act against bin Laden."

During the summer months preceding the events of September 11, 2001, Pakistan's ISI was involved in a number of nefarious activities around the world that, for the most part, should have set off alarm bells at the highest level of the U.S. government. In early June, two men, Mohammed Malik, of Pakistan, and Diaa Mohsen, an Egyptian, traveled to Florida in an attempt to purchase illegal weapons for the Taliban. What they didn't know was that they were part of a sting investigation, "Operation Diamondback," and the two were arrested and accused of attempting to buy Stinger missiles and nuclear weapons components for the ISI. Also involved in the sting were other ISI agents who attempted to pay for military weapons with heroin. Mohsen pled guilty to the charges and accepted a thirty-month stint in prison, but charges against Malik were dropped. Curiously, Malik's court files were completely sealed, and, in Mohsen's case, prosecutors "removed references to Pakistan from public filings because of diplomatic concerns." Federal agents were reportedly miffed that Washington higher-ups did not make the case more of a priority, noting that had the deal been real Osama bin Laden may have been able to acquire a nuclear bomb.

That same summer, Egyptian investigators were able to track down Ahmed al-Khadir, a close associate of bin Laden's in Pakistan. The Egyptians notified the ISI and requested their assistance in arresting al-Khadir, and the ISI leaped into action. An ISI car with diplomatic plates arrived at the safe house where al-Khadir was hiding. Inside the car were heavily armed Taliban security forces that grabbed him and whisked him back to Afghanistan, rescuing him from Egyptian prosecution.

Shortly before the attacks of 9/11, Osama bin Laden was believed to be suffering from renal deficiency and undergoing dialysis treatment in a Peshawar military hospital with the knowledge and approval of the ISI. In fact, CBS News would later report that bin Laden received emergency medical care at a military hospital in Rawalpindi, Pakistan, on September 10, 2001. Pakistani forces were said to have guarded bin Laden, and urology department staff were replaced by a secret team of medical personnel. The implications, if this story is true, are enormous, since it would appear that Pakistan could easily have detained bin Laden. According to an article in *Jane's Intelligence Digest*, "it is becoming clear that both the Taliban and al-Qaeda would have found it difficult to have continued functioning—including the latter group's terrorist activities—without substantial aid and support from Islamabad [Pakistan]."

Just three weeks before September 11, the United States was engaged in "intense negotiations" with Pakistan to establish covert actions to capture or kill Osama bin Laden. However, U.S. intelligence once again came up against the empty promises and doublespeak of the Pakistani government. According to the *Asia Times*, there was a "very strong lobby within the [Pakistani] army not to assist in any U.S. moves to apprehend bin Laden."

In the week preceding the attacks of September 11, the director of the ISI, Lieutenant General Mahmood Ahmed, came to Washington at the request of the U.S. to discuss the Osama bin Laden problem. Over several days, he met with officials from the National Security Council, CIA director George Tenet, and White House officials, and was in a meeting at the time of the attacks, which extended his trip until September 16. On September 9, just two days before the tragedy, the leader of Afghanistan's Northern Alliance, General Ahmed Shah Massoud, was assassinated by two al-Qaeda operatives who successfully posed as Moroccan journalists. The assassination was seen later as a move by the Taliban to eliminate the highly respected former mujahedeen commander before an inevitable American invasion following the events of 9/11. If true, it suggests that the Taliban had prior knowledge of the al-Qaeda attacks in the U.S.

Following the destruction of the World Trade Center in New York, talks involving Lieutenant General Mahmood took a more forceful turn. Deputy secretary of state Richard Armitage visited Mahmood and offered him a choice: "Help us and breathe in the 21st century along with the international community or be prepared to live in the Stone Age." Secretary of State Colin Powell was more specific and presented Mahmood with seven demands, delivered as an ultimatum. Pakistan supposedly agreed to all seven. Some reports suggest that Israel and India threatened to attack Pakistan and take control of its nuclear weapons if Pakistan did not side with the United States against the Taliban. Other reports suggest that Pakistan was fortunate to have Mahmood in Washington at the time, since his presence may have helped avert a war.

When Mahmood returned to Pakistan the following week, President Musharraf called a meeting with a dozen of his most senior officers, proposing that Pakistan support the United States in the impending war against bin Laden and the Taliban. Supposedly, four senior generals, in "a stunning display of disloyalty," opposed Musharraf unequivocally.

Among them was ISI Director Mahmood, who just days earlier had promised the United States full support against al-Qaeda and the Taliban. On September 17, Mahmood traveled to Kandahar, Afghanistan, with Pakistani delegates in tow, for the purpose of convincing Mullah Omar to give up bin Laden or face immediate attack by the United States. With Mahmood was Lieutenant General Muzaffar Usmani, another devout Muslim who opposed Musharraf's decision to support the United States. Both generals met with Omar, but a senior Taliban official later claimed that Mahmood urged Omar not to hand over bin Laden and promised ISI support in resisting the United States. When Musharraf learned of this insubordinance, both Mahmood and Usmani were fired. It was later learned that Mahmood had links to Saeed Sheikh and to the funding of the 9/11 attacks, and an FBI report is believed to imply that Mahmood himself may have instructed Sheikh to transfer $100,000 into hijacker Mohamed Atta's bank account before 9/11.

With the invasion of Afghanistan drawing near, the ISI, in addition to helping the Taliban devise defenses against the United States in Kandahar, was also helping terrorist groups carry out offensive strikes in Indian-controlled Kashmir. On October 1, 2001, a suicide truck bomb hit the provincial parliamentary assembly, killing thirty-six, and two of the names that surfaced as planners were Saeed Sheikh and Aftab Ansari.

Indian intelligence later claimed that they presented Musharraf with a recording of a phone call between Maulana Masood Azhar, the leader of the terrorist group Jaish-e-Mohammad, and General Mahmood, in which Azhar reported the bombing was a "success."

At that point, after being officially released from his ISI duties, Mahmood disappeared, and it is believed he is still living under virtual house arrest in Pakistan. No charges have been brought against him, and there is no evidence that the United States has sought to question him. However, stating that Mahmood is under house arrest in Pakistan is not much different than stating that "the ISI is keeping an eye on him." The same could be said of Dawood Ibrahim and Osama bin Laden, for that matter, and does little to reassure the Western world.

In late October 2001, *The Economist* reported that the Taliban were dumping their stockpile of heroin on the open market to pay for the war against the United States. There is little chance of this happening without the consent of Dawood Ibrahim and D Company. Prices fell from $700 per kilo before September 11 to just $100, and with 70 percent of the world's opium coming from Afghanistan, the street value is estimated at between $40 billion and $80 billion. After the Taliban were defeated, victorious warlords were quick to open "the Opium Floodgates," encouraging farmers to plant "as much opium as possible."

On December 13, 2001, terrorists made a daring grenade-and-rifle attack at the Indian Parliament building in New Delhi. Fourteen people, including the five attackers, were killed, and India immediately fingered Jaish-e-Mohammad, the terrorist group now funded heavily by Dawood Ibrahim. Just two weeks after the attack, Maulana Masood Azhar, the head of Jaish-e-Mohammad, was arrested by the Pakistanis and his group was outlawed. Tension between the two countries became so great that there was talk of nuclear war, and India put half a million troops on the Pakistan border. It wasn't until President Musharraf promised to crack down on terrorist groups in January 2002 that the tensions eased—for the time being. Azhar, however, was freed after a year, and it was later learned that both Sheikh and Ansari were also behind the Indian Parliament attack.

Since the war in Afghanistan, many Islamic militants have retreated into Pakistan. Some have been redirected to Kashmir, where terrorist activities continue to this day, while others have returned to villages along the Afghan/Pakistani border that have no allegiance to the government of Pakistan. This was never more evident than in late March 2004, when the Pakistan army believed it had al-Qaeda's number two operative, Ayman al-Zawahri, surrounded in South Waziristan. Fierce battles broke out between tribal warriors in the area and the Pakistan army. Al-Zawahri was never found, but the army arrested more than one hundred foreigners, including Arabs, Chechens, and Uzbeks, who were seeking refuge in Wana, Pakistan. Just days later, the Pakistan army was ambushed by tribal rebels. A dozen soldiers were killed and many more wounded. Not surprisingly, the army had discovered an elaborate tunnel system, similar to the ones in Khost, which ran for miles to remote areas along the border. It is believed that the ISI may have had a hand in the funding and constructing of such tunnels, and it is no secret that Dawood Ibrahim has taken advantage of them when smuggling drugs through the region. The CIA believes that Osama bin Laden has been able to effectively avoid capture in areas such as South Waziristan.

Shamshad Amad, Pakistan's ambassador to the United Nations and former foreign secretary, described the influence of the United States' former relationship with the ISI as having had serious consequences in the region. In an interview in 2001 he said, "After the Soviets were forced out of Afghanistan, you left us in the lurch with all the problems stemming from the war: an influx of refugees, the drug and gun runnings, a Kalashnikov culture."

It does not require much imagination to understand how a man like Dawood Ibrahim can take advantage of this situation.

"General Musharraf has made attempts to purge the Pakistan army of avowed religious hard liners. . . . The Pakistan army high command will never let politicians of any shade, especially religious ones, get anywhere near the country's nuclear assets."

–Selig S. Harrison,

director of the Center

for International Policy

CHAPTER SEVEN

PAKISTAN'S NUCLEAR SECRETS REVEALED: DAWOOD AND THE MERCHANTS OF DEATH

The news coming out of Pakistan in February 2004 was hardly a shock to Washington. Pakistani nuclear scientist and father of Pakistan's nuclear bomb Abdul Qadeer Khan had confessed to running a vast nuclear technology smuggling network for more than a decade. His motivation was greed, he admitted, and, just a week later, President Pervez Musharraf pardoned him. Musharraf had been hoping to put the whole mess behind him, issuing a series of convoluted and contradictory statements that had the universal effect of simply raising more serious questions than were answered. Since he took power in a coup in 1999, Musharraf had insisted that Pakistan's nuclear assets were completely safe, tightly controlled by the army and the ISI. Khan's admission did little to allay fears, however. Subsequent reports appear to indicate that Pakistan was well aware that Khan was passing nuclear technology through black market channels, and not all the money was going directly into Khan's pockets. Still, he was adamant about his renegade actions. In his confession to the people of Pakistan, Khan said, "There was never any kind of authorization for these activities by the government. I take full responsibility for my actions and seek your pardon."

Former Pakistani prime minister Benzir Bhutto, exiled in England, told the BBC that she believed Musharraf was engaged in a cover up. "Many of us believe that General Musharraf himself is involved," she said. "Dr. Khan could not have done this on his own. There are certainly other people involved."

Many Western diplomats and officials are not convinced Abdul Khan would have been able to sell nuclear secrets and technology without the knowledge of Pakistan's army and the ISI. Indeed, the feeling is that he was made a scapegoat to protect others and then was granted a pardon in exchange for his cooperation in the coverup. Khan's associates have insisted all along that officials were aware of, and even approved, his actions. According to UPI's Anwar Iqbal, Khan's friends and relatives told the UPI that "successive Pakistani governments had allowed him

[Khan] to indulge in this trade to raise money for the nuclear program, which cost the country about $10 billion."

In 1974, when India successfully conducted its first nuclear tests, Pakistan started a nuclear program of its own in a frantic effort to keep pace and to stave off what it perceived to be its greatest military threat. But, unlike India, Pakistan's economy would not support the vast infrastructure necessary to support a full-fledged nuclear program. So it turned to the black market, smuggling technology and equipment from all around the world. Over the years, Pakistanis often were arrested in North America and Europe trying to make illegal purchases for Pakistan's nuclear program.

A senior Pakistani official told Iqbal: "An entire system of covert operations was set up in Pakistan to build the program. Customs officials and law enforcement agencies were instructed not to open consignments and boxes coming from certain addresses or certain individuals. Khan was one of those whose consignments were never opened."

Immediately following the announcement that Dr. Khan had been arrested for selling nuclear secrets, his daughter, Dina, fled Pakistan, reportedly carrying incriminating documents and a videotape that differs from the confession her father delivered on Pakistani television. It is believed that the papers may reveal exactly what Pakistani military officials knew about the situation, and Dina may be safeguarding them to prevent any "unfortunate accidents" that may befall Dr. Khan.

Curiously, President Musharraf has made no effort to seize any of Khan's assets from his illegal profiteering. "He can keep his money," Musharraf said. "We wanted the bomb in the national interest, and so you have to ask yourself whether you act against the person who enabled you to get the bomb." He then went on to say, "Obviously, we made our nuclear strength from the underworld. We did not buy openly. Every single atomic power has come through the underworld, even India."

As expected, the United States threw their support behind Musharraf. Foreign Ministry spokesman Masood Khan said that U.S. Secretary of State Colin Powell had spoken to President Musharraf and Musharraf had "conveyed Pakistan's firm resolve that such activity will never happen in the future." Khan also said that Powell assured Musharraf that the United States "will continue to support international efforts to curb proliferation."

At least, that was the public spin on the discussion. Behind the scenes, there was much speculation among U.S. officials about how Khan's confession might be just the tip of the iceberg, and there was no telling how large this "underground nuclear supermarket" had grown. The UN International Atomic Energy Agency (IAEA) had uncovered a sprawling black market, dominated by Pakistani involvement with Libya, Iran, and North Korea. But the abundance of nuclear "middlemen" almost had ensured that there were numerous other countries involved, and there were no guarantees that all customers in the nuclear black market game were governments.

So just who are these middlemen who enable countries such as Pakistan, Libya, Iran, and North Korea to trade in nuclear technology? And what other organizations have the motivation and the money to purchase enriched uranium and other nuclear technologies? If Dawood Ibrahim has offered the ISI use of his shipping and smuggling routes to help procure nuclear materials for Pakistan, what would stop him from making similar deals for himself—perhaps to ensure that D Company or Lashkar-e-Toiba are more dangerously armed than their rivals? Some of the men who trade in the nuclear black market are among the most dangerous in the world—loyal only to the highest bidder. To date, Pakistan has played the black market better than any of its 1998 nuclear tests show, which has gone a long way toward neutralizing India's advantage in the region. But at what cost?

In 2002, General Musharraf referred to extremists within Pakistan's borders and their "half-baked religious minds." He had two thousand of the country's most extreme militants jailed, much to the pleasure of India and the West, who had long complained that Pakistan was a country that its government had no authority over. The problem, however, is that moves like this appear to offer only temporary appeasement. Months later, most of the militants were released from prison—including, according to Rory McArthy, many heads of terrorist groups—because they were necessary in Kashmir's struggle against India. Pakistan's ISI does not back Musharraf one hundred percent, especially given the country's support of the United States in the war against terror. And because the ISI has a significant number of Islamic militants high up in its ranks, not every action the ISI engages in is necessarily in Pakistan's best interest. It came as no surprise to Musharraf that two recent assassination attempts on his life, just weeks apart, originated in the Islamic militant community, and, as with everything in Pakistan, one had to wonder about the ISI connections. As long as the ISI continues to employ Islamic militants and known terrorists, Pakistan is going to remain unstable, despite the best efforts of the West to support Musharraf. And despite Musharraf's claims that Pakistan's nuclear assets are tightly controlled by the army, the fact remains that the sordid nature of the key players in the nuclear black market ensures that nuclear technology simply cannot be tightly controlled.

In any intelligence report about the nuclear black market, one man's name comes up again and again as a high-powered broker of nuclear technologies: Bukhary Seyed Abu Tahir, a Sri Lankan businessman who now makes Malaysia his home, caught the attention of the White House recently, and President Bush referred to him as the "chief financial officer and money launderer" of A. Q. Khan's nuclear operations.

Tahir was born in Tamil Nadu, India, on April 17, 1959, and his family moved to Sri Lanka when he was five. After attending school in India, Tahir and his brother, Seyed Ibrahim Bukhary, helped their father establish the Dubai-based company SMB Computers. It was at SMB that the Tahirs met Dr. Khan through an uncle and began to help the Pakistani scientist in his "proliferation activities."

When Tahir's father passed away in 1985, B.S.A. Tahir took over the management of SMB, and he began visiting Pakistan on a regular basis. At first, his involvement mostly centered on arranging legitimate contracts, such as selling air-conditioning equipment to Khan's laboratories. But it is believed that by 1994, Tahir, who had already begun manufacturing centrifuges for uranium enrichment plants, was asked by Pakistani officials to ship two containers of used centrifuge units from Pakistan to Iran. Taking advantage of the liberal record-keeping protocol in Dubai, Tahir was said to receive suitcases full of millions of U.S. dollars as payment for these transactions. Dawood Ibrahim had long ago set up shipping businesses in Dubai for these very reasons. According to an Op-Ed piece by Gary Milhollin and Kelly Motz, Dubai may be "the easiest place in the world to mask the real destination of cargo." Tahir continued these shipments right up until Khan's confession in February 2004.

Pakistan's involvement in these sales was headed by Major

General Sultan Habib, an ISI officer in charge of the "clandestine procurement of nuclear and missile technology" from abroad. Remarkably, Tahir's family was very close to Dawood Ibrahim, who, it is believed, loaned Pakistan the money on numerous occasions to conduct these nuclear transactions. Dawood had many of his own established shipping routes from his real estate, hawala, and shipping businesses in Singapore and Malaysia, and it is believed he helped facilitate many of the deals with B.S.A. Tahir on Pakistan's behalf. Dawood is known to have stayed in Malaysia as a guest of Tahir's on at least one occasion in 2001, with the ISI secretly arranging for his safe passage.

One reason why the United States might be reluctant to put more intense pressure on Pakistan and the United Arab Emirates for their participation in these nuclear scandals is that, all along, Pakistan has been saying it needs to develop a more sophisticated, state-of-the-art nuclear weapons program not to keep pace with India, but rather to neutralize India's advantage. In March 2004, Pakistan tested a nuclear-capable missile called "Shaheen II," which has the potential for carrying both nuclear and conventional warheads deep into India. The test of the Shaheen II was viewed as a political statement both to reassure Pakistanis that, after the Khan scandal, the country's nuclear program was still healthy, and to show neighbors, mainly India, that its program was progressing.

Pakistan used the nuclear black market to build its nuclear

program because sanctions against the country prohibited the legitimate purchase of enriched uranium and other nuclear technology. Yet fear that Pakistan's nuclear weapons will fall into the hands of terrorists or Islamic militants is a topic that is constantly in the news in South Asia. Indeed, immediately following the events of September 11, a secret plan between India and Israel was devised wherein commando units would conduct a surprise raid to secure Pakistan's nuclear facilities to prevent them from falling into the hands of extremists and forces loyal to the Taliban in Afghanistan. In an article on Newsmax.com, Ahmar Mustikhan quotes the prominent U.S. Asia expert and director of the Center for International Policy, Selig S. Harrison, as saying, "General Musharraf has made attempts to purge the Pakistan army of avowed religious hard liners...The Pakistan army high command will never let politicians of any shade, especially religious ones, get anywhere near the country's nuclear assets."

Is it necessary that Islamic militants or terrorist groups come into possession of nuclear warheads to advance their causes? Most experts believe no. In fact, precedent has it that the elements of a "dirty bomb" would be far more useful to *jihadis* and terrorist groups. Radiological dispersion bombs, or dirty bombs, may consist of any radiological waste or by-products from a nuclear reactor packaged together with conventional explosives, resulting in a detonation that would scatter deadly radioactive particles into the vicinity. While actual nuclear weapons are heavily guarded, radioactive waste can be obtained around the world—and nowhere is it easier than in India, Pakistan, and Russia.

In 1996, Islamic militants from Chechnya, the province that broke from the Soviet Union, managed to obtain enough radioactive waste to assemble a dirty bomb. The rebels planted the bomb in the center of Izmailovo Park in Moscow but did not detonate it, as a statement to Russia about its vulnerability to such an attack. In January 2004, the U.S. Senate Foreign Relations Committee met to specifically address the danger of dirty bombs in South Asia. Political analyst and founder of the Henry L. Stimson Center think tank Michael Krepon described a nightmare scenario, concluding that both India and Pakistan were "very vulnerable" to a dirty bomb attack. "The first act of nuclear terrorism will be a momentously bad event," he told the committee. "In tense regions like South Asia, the detonation of a 'dirty bomb' could scuttle a peace process and generate severe pressures for escalation." Senator Joseph Biden said he was concerned about the impact a dirty bomb would have in South Asia, and suggested that the United States should be "extremely proactive" in offering help to both New Delhi and Islamabad. Senate Foreign Relations Committee chairman Richard Lugar said that the stakes had become too high to risk a return to military confrontation or the creation of new sources of Islamic terrorism.

The threat, according to many experts, has progressed so far beyond the hypothetical and into the "only a matter of time" category that cities around the world are training police and hospitals in how to deal with a dirty bomb attack. The British Broadcasting Corporation reported in January 2003 that al-Qaeda had already built a crude radiological device. At one point, British intelligence agents infiltrated the network and learned that Osama bin Laden's terrorist network put such a device together in Herat—an area of western Afghanistan. It has long been known that al-Qaeda has wanted to acquire and develop a nuclear weapon, and it is believed that the Taliban regime assisted al-Qaeda in the construction of this dirty bomb, which has not been recovered. Computer hard drives recovered by U.S. troops and journalists during the 2001 war in Afghanistan included files that showed al-Qaeda's interest in being able to use these weapons of mass destruction against the West. In fact, during a trial that stemmed from the bombings of two U.S. Embassies in Africa, Jamal Ahmed al-Fadi, a former aide to bin Laden, testified that he was ordered in 1993 to buy uranium on the black market for a nuclear weapon. Al-Fadi said that al-Qaeda was prepared to spend over $1.5 million on such a purchase, but he was unaware if one was ever made.

In June 2003, the head of Britain's MI5 warned that it was

"only a matter of time" before al-Qaeda terrorists launched some kind of nuclear, chemical, or biological attack on a Western city. The director of the Security Service, Eliza Manningham-Buller, said "renegade scientists"—understood to be from Pakistan—had provided Islamic militants information to create weapons of mass destruction, specifically dirty bombs, and, in her opinion, these weapons would only get more sophisticated as time went on. She stated: "We are faced with a realistic possibility of a form of unconventional attack that could include chemical, biological, radiological or nuclear."

So concerned was the United States with the prospect of a Pakistan-linked terrorist using a dirty bomb that in June of 2002 federal officials captured Jose Padilla, a U.S. citizen who was suspected of having ties to al-Qaeda and was allegedly planning to build and explode a radioactive bomb in the United States. Padilla, also believed to be known as Abdullah al-Muhajir, was arrested at Chicago's O'Hare Airport when he was tracked flying between Pakistan, Egypt, and Switzerland. He was treated as an "enemy combatant" of the United States after a captured al-Qaeda figure, Abu Zubaydah, spoke to authorities about Padilla. In December 2003, however, a federal appeals court ordered Padilla's release from military custody, stating that "The president's inherent constitutional powers do not extend to the detention as an enemy combatant of an American citizen seized within the country away from a zone of combat."

Pakistan is estimated to possess between thirty and fifty atomic bombs, with explosive yields ranging from 1 to 15 kilotons. According to Bruce G. Blair, president of the Center for Defense Information, Pakistan's nuclear weapons are probably assembled at Wah, which is about fifty miles from Afghanistan, and are stored primarily at Sargodha, near a missile complex close to the Indian border. Blair wrote: "Pakistan's military government is walking a tightrope between pressure from the Bush administration on one side and anti-American Islamic militants on the other. Growing street opposition from the latter could certainly de-stabilize or even topple the regime, and in the midst of such dissolution, the weakening of nuclear security would inevitably occur."

Bruce Blair goes on to state that the ranks of Pakistan's government and military personnel are laden with sympathizers of the radical Islamic faction (including the ISI), which poses the threat of "insiders colluding to spirit away a bomb or two for bin Laden or other terrorists."

In sum, Pakistan clearly is in the forefront when it comes to concern about nuclear terrorism. And why not. Pakistan provided safe haven to the Osama bin Ladens and Dawood Ibrahims of the world. Its intelligence agency is riddled with Islamic militant sympathizers and known operatives from some of the deadliest terror organizations in the world. It is a country that has in its possession a number of atomic bombs, and a significant percentage of its population would just as soon see President Musharraf dead and Pakistan's alliance with the West dropped. It is easy to see why the United States has to tread carefully in this region. In Musharraf, the United States has found a leader who, for the most part, is willing to stand up to Islamic fundamentalists and support U.S. efforts against terror. But in order to keep Musharraf in power, the United States has been forced at times to look the other way when the ISI chooses to harbor men like Dawood Ibrahim within its borders. It is a deadly and dangerous game in the most dangerous part of the world, and, time and again, the United States has witnessed its perceived "friends" in this region turn against them at the drop of a hat.

"In a post-extradition pact scenario, either the ISI will liquidate Dawood camouflaging it as internecine gang rivalry or keep him and his movements under tight surveillance."

–Dossier on Dawood Ibrahim, Union Home Ministry (India)

CONCLUSION:

DAWOOD IBRAHIM'S FINAL STAND

The October 2003 announcement by the United States Treasury Department designating Dawood Ibrahim as a global terrorist has, despite his billions and a security force to rival any world leader, made life more difficult for the King of Karachi. In fact, reports out of Pakistan have the former Bombay mafia don being moved between Karachi and Islamabad on a regular basis ever since the United States linked him to Osama bin Laden. According to Vijay Dutt, Dawood has been increasingly worried about his safety since November 2003, when he learned of investigations into Dr. Abdul Qadeer Khan's selling of nuclear weapons technology in the black market. "The report that Dr. Khan was in critical condition after a sudden heart attack or even the amended report that he was in very bad health must have made the ever suspicious

Dawood even more concerned."

Dutt writes that Dawood has reportedly been undergoing plastic surgery to alter his appearance, sensing that the end may be near and he will be forced to flee Pakistan. Others believe Dawood will never be permitted to leave Pakistan alive. A more likely scenario is that he will be either contained in Pakistan or simply killed. Like Dr. Khan, Dawood clearly knows much more about Pakistan's cooperation in black market dealings than he is willing to admit, and the ISI could not chance Dawood being turned over to India because he would surely embarrass Pakistan by detailing ISI's involvement in suspect activities.

Dawood Ibrahim is feeling the heat. According to Siddharth Srivastava, reports have Dawood's personal security guards— "the cream of Pakistan's Inter-Services Intelligence (ISI) agency"—being removed. President Musharraf is beginning to insist on some kind of crackdown on Dawood in an effort to improve Indo-Pak relations and appease the United States after the Khan nuclear scandal. "If Dawood is nabbed, it will be the biggest step Pakistan undertakes to curb cross-border terrorism on the eastern side of the border," said an official with the Foreign Ministry.

Ghulam Hasnain's story, which peaked the interest of reporter Daniel Pearl, detailed the life and times of the man living as the King of Karachi. Still, Hasnain wrote about the nostalgia Dawood feels for the India that he left behind, and it is said that Dawood often cries for Bombay. "Bombay was Bombay," one of Dawood's associates said. "There we had everything. Here one cannot have the life or the fun we did in India."

With his Karachi life, as some believe, nearing the end, Dawood Ibrahim has been reported to do what millions around the world do every day: use the Internet to keep up with friends and family he may never see again. According to Ashwini Bhatnagar, Dawood adopted the screen name *Janu*, an Urdu term for "lovey-dovey" that is derived from the word *jaan*, meaning "life." It is with a bit of irony, Bhatnagar writes, "the term is just as apt as Dawood mostly deals out either life or death. The latter more so if one fails to warm the cockles of his heart." Dawood also listed himself in his profile as a "self-employed businessman" and used "Bombay" as his password—indication that he truly may be nostalgic for home.

In a story by S. Hussain Zaidi, the author speculated that Dawood Ibrahim might even try to return to India voluntarily. According to a crime branch officer who once arrested Dawood in Bombay, "It is highly unlikely that Dawood will return to India, but if he has to lead a prisoner's life in Pakistan, he might decide to live the same kind of life here too." In fact, the Union Home Ministry of India released a new dossier on Dawood that basically conceded the fact that the underworld don was never going to be extradited from Pakistan. It even suggested that

India drop Ibrahim's name from the list of twenty criminals India believes are avoiding prosecution by hiding in Pakistan. The dossier also included a line that may explain his decision to have his face altered by plastic surgery: ". . . in a post-extradition pact scenario, either the ISI will liquidate Dawood camouflaging it as internecine gang rivalry or keep him and his movements under tight surveillance."

According to Zaidi, Dr. Satyapal Singh, Bombay joint commissioner of police, agrees: "After the treaty, he will have outlived his resourcefulness for Pakistani operatives. So he will either be conveniently eliminated or confined so that their secret remains a secret forever."

Dubai, once a haven for Dawood Ibrahim, is no longer an option. The UAE has been trying to shed its "mafia haven" reputation, and he has been selling off his businesses and assets there over the past year. Chhota Rajan finally received a measure of revenge against Ibrahim when he had Sharad Shetty, one of Ibrahim's high-ranking aides, gunned down outside his offices in 2003. The blow was a crippling one for Dawood that he has been unable to recover from, since Shetty ran his empire in Dubai.

It is difficult to imagine a life on the run for the man who, as Hasnain wrote, is accustomed to a daily swim in his palatial swimming pool, games of cricket or snooker in the afternoon, Black Label scotch in the evening, and the company of the finest virgins money can buy. Dawood Ibrahim has spent his whole life building and nurturing this decadent lifestyle. Unlike Osama bin Laden, who is willing to live in dark, cold caves to facilitate his jihad against the West, Dawood has always been about self-preservation without sacrifice. In the past when he has felt the heat, he's bought his way into comfort and befriended his host countries in mutually beneficial ways. But since the events of September 11, the world is getting smaller for him. Is Dawood capable of a dangerous final stand? Through all his nefarious activities and connections, is it possible he's saved for himself weapons of mass destruction to be used in a desperate situation? One would assume that the Pakistanis have considered this and that it might be part of the reason he is permitted to stay and thus far survive. After all, the ISI knows better than anyone that, after masterminding the Bombay serial blasts, he can be ruthless when it comes to revenge. And he actually showed restraint on that Black Friday in Bombay. He could have easily arranged far greater destruction to the people of his home city, and it would be foolish for them to think he couldn't turn on Pakistan at any moment.

ENDNOTES

INTRODUCTION
They wouldn't dare refuse: *Newsline*, September 2001.
more loyal to Dawood: Ibid.

1. THE KING OF KARACHI
According to Robert Sam Anson: "The Journalist and the Terrorist," *Vanity Fair*, August 2002.
A few days later: Ibid.
It is believed: Ahmar Mustikhan, Newsmax.com, March 14, 2002.
According to Siddharth Varadarajan: Times News Network, March 11, 2002.
I know people in the government: Anson, "The Journalist and the Terrorist."
We can only presume: Varadarajan, Times News Network.
That same day: *The Economic Times*, October 18, 2003.
The CIA had already gathered unassailable evidence: Newsmax.com, June 4, 2003.
According to an article by B. Raman: "Musharraf's Nucleargate," February 23, 2004.

4. MAFIA WARS
Our idea was to capture him: Interview with Sheela Bhatt, *Asia Times*, September 15, 2000.
But soon, according to S. Hussain Zaidi: "Gangsta' Rap: The Life and Times of Chhota Rajan," September 24, 2000.
Our idea was to capture him alive: Bhatt, *Asia Times*.
I am in Europe: *Star News*, December 6, 2000.
According to a story by Bertil Lintner: *The Week*, December 10, 2000.
Chhota Shakeel, in an interview with Sheela Raval: *India Today*, January 2001.
According to Shakeel: Ibid.
Shakeel told Raval: *The Nation*, February 15, 1999.

5. DAWOOD IBRAHIM AND PAKISTAN'S ISI

Shortly after Ibrahim left Dubai for Karachi: *Frontline* magazine, February 2002.

Dawood, as Hasnain reported: *Newsline*, September 2001.

And the overwhelming amount of money and weapons: *The Nation*, February 15, 1999.

If their local allies were involved: Alfred McCoy, *The Politics of Heroin*, Chicago Review Press, 1991.

There is some speculation: Sunday *Times*, August 25, 2002.

By 1984, bin Laden left Saudi Arabia: *The New Yorker*, January 24, 2000.

Money made from smuggling drugs: *Financial Times*, August 10, 2001.

invisible government: *Time*, May 6, 2002.

In Pakistan, tens of thousands: *Washington Post*, July 19, 2002.

But the CIA was beginning to sense a turning of the tide: *Newsweek*, September 24, 2001.

The consequences for all of us are astronomical: *Atlantic Monthly*, May 1996.

For more than seven years: *The Nation*, February 15, 1999.

BCCI did dirty work: *Los Angeles Times*, January 20, 2002.

6. THE PATH TO 9/11

The supposedly devout Muslim: *Los Angeles Times*, June 24, 2002.

What is known: *Times* (London), November 10, 2002.

There is a clear operational link: *Los Angeles Times*, December 22, 2002.

It was later learned: *Los Angeles Times*, February 9, 2002.

Some of the profits: *India Today*, February 14, 2002.

It was around this time: Sunday *Times*, April 21, 2002.

I have come here: Associated Press, January 5, 2000.

my special son: Robert Sam Anson, *Vanity Fair*, August 2002.

It is interesting to note: State Department Fact Sheet, December 11, 2001.

is believed to have been given a house by the ISI: Anson, *Vanity Fair*.

Because he was able to help al-Qaeda: Ibid.

He was working alongside: *New York Times*, February 25, 2002.

It is around this time: *Telegraph*, September 30, 2001.

According to a story in the *New York Times*: October 29, 2001.

and experts at the time: CNN, October 5, 1996.

I warned them: James Risen and Judith Miller, *New York Times*, October 29, 2001.

The Taliban are not just recruits: *Times of India*, March 7, 2001.

Despite their clean chins: *Wall Street Journal*, November 15, 2001.

Al-Qaeda had assumed control: *Los Angeles Times*, November 18, 2001.

The Afghans taxed the opium production: *Washington Post*, February 17, 2002.

not wanting to offend an ally: *Los Angeles Times*, November 18, 2001.

However, in October 1996: *The Guardian*, April 17, 2002.

He delivered at least forty tons: Ibid.

A few years later: *Montreal Gazette*, February 5, 2002.

However, Bout was suspected: *The Guardian*, April 17, 2002.

Yoseff Bodansky: *Star Tribune*, September 30, 2001.

If accurate: *Financial Times*, November 28, 2001.

After the bombing, President Clinton claimed: *The New Yorker*, January 24, 2000.

A U.S. defense analyst said: *Washington Post*, October 3, 2001.

Alex Standish: *Jane's Intelligence Review*, October 5, 2001.

In early June, two men: *Washington Post*, August 2, 2002.

Also involved in the sting: *New York Times*, June 16, 2001.

removed references to Pakistan: *Washington Post*, August 2, 2002.

Federal agents were reportedly miffed: Ibid.

That same summer: *Time*, May 6, 2002.

In fact, CBS News would later report: January 28, 2002.

According to an article in *Jane's Intelligence Digest*: September 20, 2001.

According to the *Asia Times*: August 22, 2001.

In the week preceding the attacks: *The News*, September 10, 2001.

If true: *Time*, August 4, 2002.

Help us: Deutsche Press-Agentur, September 12, 2001.

Pakistan supposedly agreed to all seven: *Washington Post*, January 29, 2002.

Some reports suggest: *LA Weekly*, November 9, 2002.

Other reports: *Financial Times*, September 18, 2002.

Among them: *The Guardian*, May 25, 2002.

Both generals met with Omar: *Associated Press*, February 21, 2002.

It was later learned: *Times of India*, October 9, 2002.

On October 1, 2001: *Vanity Fair*, August 2002.

Indian intelligence later claimed: United Press International, October 10, 2001.

At that point, after being officially released: *Asia Times*, January 5, 2002.

Prices fall from $700 per kilo: *The Economist*, October 18, 2001.

Once the fighting began in Afghanistan: *The Observer*, November 25, 2001.

It wasn't until President Musharraf: *Wall Street Journal*, January 2, 2002.

Sheikh and Ansari were also behind the Indian Parliament attack: *Vanity Fair*, August 2002.

Shamshad Amad, Pakistan's ambassador: *New York Times*, October 29, 2001.

7. PAKISTAN'S NUCLEAR SECRETS REVEALED

General Musharraf has made attempts: Ahmar Mustikhan, Newsmax.com, June 4, 2003.

According to UPI's Anwar Iqbal: *Washington Times*, February 18, 2004.

Over the years, Pakistanis often were arrested: Ibid.

He can keep his money: *Sunday Telegraph*, February 8, 2004.

Obviously, we made our nuclear strength from the underworld: Ibid.

Foreign Ministry spokesman Masood Khan: *Agence France-Presse*, February 8, 2004.

Behind the scenes: "Questions Over Pakistan Gov't Role in Nuke Scandal," Reuters, February 4, 2004.

according to Rory McArthy: "Dangerous Game of State-Sponsored Terror That Threatens Nuclear Conflict," *Guardian Unlimited*, May 25, 2002.

Tahir was born: "Musharraf's Nucleargate," South Asia Analysis Group, February 23, 2004.

It was at SMB: Ibid.

But it is believed: Ibid.

According to an Op-Ed piece by Gary Milhollin and Kelly Motz: *New York Times*, March 4, 2004.

Pakistan's involvement in these sales: South Asia Analysis Group, February 23, 2004.

In an article on Newsmax.com: "Pakistan Looms as Nuclear Menace," June 4, 2002.

Political analyst and founder: India Express Bureau, January 29, 2004.

Senator Joseph Biden: Ibid.

The director of Security Service: "Matter of Time Before Dirty Bomb Attack, Says MI5 Chief," *The Independent*, June 18, 2003.

According to Bruce G. Blair: *What If the Terrorists Go Nuclear?*, CDI, October 1, 2001.

CONCLUSION

According to Vijay Dutt: *Hindustan Times*, February 16, 2004.

According to Siddharth Srivastava: *Asia Times*, February 27, 2004.

If Dawood is nabbed: *Hindustan Times*, February 16, 2004.

Ghulam Hasnain's story: "Portrait of a Don," *Newsline*, March 17, 2004.

Bombay was Bombay: Ibid.

According to Ashwini Bhatnagar: "Dusk Descends on Don," *India Tribune*, February 3, 2002.

In a story by S. Hussain Zaidi: *Mid-Day Bombay*, February 6, 2004.

In fact, the Union Home Ministry: Ibid.

in a post-extradition pact scenario: Ibid.